Lessons
from the
Life of
Moody

Lessons from the Life of Moody

by

George Sweeting
and
Donald Sweeting

MOODY PRESS
CHICAGO

Affectionately dedicated to all our brothers and sisters who by faith are the heirs of D. L. Moody.

May the Lord give to each employee and associate of the Moody Bible Institute of Chicago a commitment to Christ and the compassion of our founder, D. L. Moody.

Contents

Foreword

Some few lives cast long shadows of impact—impact for Christ and eternity that stretches far beyond the brief span of their own existence. Such was the life of Dwight Lyman Moody. Common—to some even crude—energetic, and totally committed to Christ, this shoe-salesman-turned-evangelist was used of God in stellar proportions.

Men like D. L. Moody intrigue me. Their unique place in Christ's kingdom lifts them up as almost mythological heroes. We stand in awe, never dreaming to be used as they were.

Yet after reading this account of D. L. Moody's life, I am struck with the reality of God's desire to use people, even the unsophisticated, if they will simply yield and serve without distraction. A love for God. A passion for the lost. A will to be used. Those are the basic essentials, and they come together in an unusual way in Mr. Moody.

The research of Dr. Sweeting and his son Don leaves us with a clear and inspiring glimpse of Mr. Moody. This book modifies the myth and presents our hero in the light of who he really was: an authentic, balanced, passionate, uneducated, and aggressive soldier of Christ.

I know of no one more qualified to catch the spirit and character of D. L. Moody than George Sweeting. Not only has he been the steward of Moody's legacy at the Moody Bible Institute, but he has studied our hero, traveled his crusade routes, immersed himself in documents pertaining to his life, and, frequently, visited Northfield, Massachusetts, Moody's boyhood home. Dr. Sweeting is a man like Moody. He has Moody's passion for the lost, love for preaching, principles of righteous living, and persistent management of God's work entrusted to him. Dwight Moody would be pleased to know George Sweeting and be pleased to have him and his son as the authors of this work.

This book gives me hope. Hope that in some measure the simple, yet pervasive, qualities of D. L. Moody might rub off on me—and on all who read this book; hope that we, too, may be specially used of God in our own place. In God's own way.

JOSEPH M. STOWELL III

Preface

The name "Moody" is famous throughout the evangelical world—not primarily because of Moody Broadcasting Network, Moody Press, *Moody Monthly* magazine, Moody films, Moody Church, or even Moody Bible Institute, but because of D. L. Moody himself. Almost a century after his death, his life and ministry have enormous appeal.

Associate Emma Dryer called him "a divinely equipped flying artillery on life's battlefield."[1] Though untrained and unordained, this layman has been called the most famous clergyman of the nineteenth century. The *Encyclopaedia Britannica* refers to Moody as "the greatest of modern evangelists."[2]

William Garden Blaikie, professor of apologetics and pastoral theology at New College, Edinburgh, summed up Moody's ministry this way: "Mr. Moody's power as a speaker lies in his being down-right earnest. He believes what he says; he says it as if he believed it, and he expects his audience to believe it. He gets wonderfully near to his hearers, without any apparent effort. He is gifted with a rare sagacity, an insight into the human heart, a knowledge of what is stirring in it and what is fitted to impress it."[3]

Unquestionably, D. L. Moody possessed a great love for people and was able to communicate that love individually and collectively. God's love was the theme of all

1. Letter from Emma Dryer to Charles Blanchard (president of Wheaton College), January 1916, Moody Archives, p. 25.
2. *Encyclopaedia Britannica*, 1953 ed., s.v. "Moody, Dwight Lyman."
3. William G. Blaikie, *The Religious Awakening in Edinburgh* (Manchester, England, 1874), p. 4.

he believed and did. Never satisfied with the status quo, he was ever seeking for and experimenting with new ways to reach the masses.

Moody is credited with establishing three schools, a church, a publishing house, and a Bible conference. He was co-founder of the Student Volunteer Movement and is reputed to have originated the forerunner of a group active during the War Between the States, the United Servicemen's Organization.

Moody's life and work present an attractive, dynamic illustration of what God can do in the life of a person fully committed to Him. The lessons in these chapters are for each of us to observe and apply. May God refresh and renew each reader through the pages of this book.

Sincere appreciation is expressed to Beth Jesel for her hours of typing these chapters; to Dr. Joseph Stowell and Dr. Howard Whaley for their input and interest; and to Mr. Walter Osborn, Reference Librarian at the Moody Bible Institute, for his assistance in the research necessary to the preparation of this book.

GEORGE SWEETING
DONALD W. SWEETING

CHAPTER 1

D. L. Moody's Conversion

His sermons were colloquial, simple, full of conviction and point. In his theology he laid stress on the Gospel, not on sectarian opinions. His intense sympathy for, and insight into the individual, his infinite practical skill and tact, his genius for organization, his honesty, his singular largeness and sweetness of spirit and his passion for mending and winning souls made him, in spite of his scholastic defects, one of the greatest of modern evangelists.
—Encyclopaedia Britannica *(1953 edition)*

Embarrassed! That's how the New England country boy Dwight L. Moody must have felt upon entering a Sunday school class in Boston's Mount Vernon Congregational Church. After all, some of his fellow students were from Harvard College. When the teacher, Edward Kimball, asked his students to turn to the lesson in John's gospel, young Moody began fumbling around in the Old Testament. Kimball tactfully offered Moody his own Bible, which was opened to the right place.

Kimball was patient with this new member of his class. And rightly so. Young Dwight Moody obviously lacked the advantages of his "fellow scholars." Moody's formal education was minimal. When Dwight had been only four years old, his father died, bankrupt. Helping support the family meant that young Moody would have to sacrifice his public schooling.

Moody fared no better with Christian education. His home held few books, and the Bible his family did have was not a familiar book to him, despite his mother's best efforts. Teaching at the local Unitarian Church was

13

sporadic and weak. J. C. Pollock comments, "Everett the minister was a pious, kindly man, a widow's friend, and his Unitarianism was moderate (he baptized the Moodys at one batch in 1842, in the name of the Trinity he denied)."[1] However, young D. L. found church to be cold, dull, boring, and even irksome.

In March of 1854, young Moody left his Northfield, Massachusetts, home to find a job in Boston. There his uncle, Samuel Socrates Holton, after much persuasion, agreed to employ him in his prosperous shoe and boot business, but with the condition that Dwight must attend the Mount Vernon Congregational Church and Sunday school.

Sitting under the preaching of pastor Edward Kirk, Moody for the first time heard sermons that focused on Jesus Christ and His atoning work on the cross. It was a refreshing change from the passionless orthodoxy of most New England Trinitarian churches or the dry, ethical preaching of the Unitarians.

Moody later told of the impact that Kirk's preaching had on him:

> One day I was in the gallery, sound asleep . . . [when] a young student from Harvard . . . gave me a punch with his elbow and I rubbed my eyes and woke up. I looked at the minister, and lo and behold, I thought he was preaching directly at me. I said to myself, "Who has been telling Dr. Kirk about me?" The perspiration stood out all over me. I never felt so cheap in all my life. . . . At the conclusion . . . I pulled my coat collar up and got out as quick as I could."[2]

When Moody began to understand the meaning of the gospel, his first reaction was to delay—to wait until

1. J. C. Pollock, *Moody: A Biographical Portrait* (New York: Macmillan, 1963), p. 5.
2. William R. Moody, *The Life of D. L. Moody* (New York: Macmillan, 1930), p. 41.

he was an old man and then become a Christian. He said, "I thought if I had . . . some lingering disease, I would have plenty of time to become one and, in the meantime, I would enjoy the pleasures of the world."[3]

But the battle in Moody's mind and soul grew more intense with each passing week. During the month of April 1855, some of the walls of resistance began to crumble. The church was holding "revival" meetings. Everyone, including Mr. Kimball, was thinking about sharing the way of salvation with the unconverted. Kimball first thought of the boys in his Sunday school class.

Kimball recalls:

> I determined to speak to [Moody] about Christ and about his soul, and started down to Holton's shoe store. When I was nearly there I began to wonder whether I ought to go in just then during business hours. I thought that possibly my call might embarrass the boy, and that when I went away the other clerks would ask who I was, and taunt him with my efforts in trying to make him a good boy. In the meantime, I had passed the store, and discovering this, I determined to make a dash for it and have it over at once.
>
> I found Moody at the back part of the building wrapping up shoes. I went up to him at once, and putting my hand up to his shoulder, I made what I afterward felt was a very weak plea for Christ. I don't know just what words I used, nor could Mr. Moody tell. I simply told him of Christ's love for him and the love Christ wanted in return. That was all there was. It seemed the young man was just ready for the light that then broke upon him, and there, in the back of that store in Boston, he gave himself and his life to Christ.[4]

3. Pollock, *Moody*, p. 23.
4. William R. Moody, *Moody*, p. 41.

This event became the great turning point in Moody's life. Up to this time he had known only a passive religion, but not an active faith in Christ. He had understood Christ's ethics, but not Christ's power to change and sustain a life. Moody said, "Before my conversion I worked towards the cross, but since then I have worked from the cross; then I worked to be saved, now I work because I am saved."[5]

When Moody committed his life to Jesus Christ there were few outward changes. But there was a growing desire to know God in a personal way. Moody knew there was a new Presence in his life. He said, "The impulse of a converted soul is to love." And again, "The morning I was converted I went outdoors and fell in love with everything. I never loved the bright sun shining over the earth so much before, and when I heard the birds singing their sweet songs, I fell in love with the birds. Everything was different."[6]

Moody did not live in the past, though. He was more interested in looking to the future and growing as a Christian. He had an increasing desire to care for the souls of others and to master the contents of the Bible.

At times progress was painfully slow. Shortly after his conversion, he applied for membership in the Mount Vernon church, only to be turned down by the board due to his poor understanding of basic Christian doctrine.

Once again, Moody was embarrassed. Here's what was recorded in the minutes of the official church board.

> Dwight L. Moody . . . has been baptized. First awakened on the 16th day of May. Became anxious about himself. Saw himself a sinner, and sin now

5. Ibid.
6. Ibid.

seems hateful and holiness desirable. Thinks he has repented; has purposed to give up sin; feels dependent upon Christ for forgiveness. Loves the Scriptures. Prays. Desires to be useful. Religiously educated. Been in the city a year. From Northfield, this State. Not ashamed to be known as a Christian. Eighteen years old.

At this examination, however, it was believed that the applicant was not sufficiently instructed in Christian doctrine to be taken into membership. In answer to the question, "What has Christ done for you, and for us all that especially entitles Him to our love and obedience?" young Moody replied, "I think He has done a great deal for us all, but I don't know of anything He has done in particular."[7]

Because of Moody's weak response, the committee deferred recommending him for admission to church membership, but three of their number were appointed to care for him and explain to him more perfectly the way of eternal life.[8]

Moody's disastrous interview may have been caused by fear; nevertheless, he persevered and eventually was accepted and signed the membership rolls one year later, on May 3, 1856.[9]

Moody was about five feet seven inches tall, with broad, sloping shoulders; soft, gray eyes; rich, dark brown hair; and plenty of muscle and energy. Edward Kimball commented that though D. L. was warm and likable, he had never met anyone who knew as little about the Bible. Nevertheless, Moody was soundly converted and growing.

7. Ibid., pp. 43-44.
8. Ibid.
9. James F. Findlay, Jr., *Dwight L. Moody, American Evangelist* (Chicago: U. of Chicago Press, 1969).

However, shortly after his admission to the Mount Vernon Church, young Moody felt the urge to travel West to be part of the adventure and expansion of the new city of Chicago (in 1856 the population was 100,000 people).

It was September 15, 1856, at age nineteen, when young Moody bought his train ticket for five dollars. He boarded the train in Fitchburg, Massachusetts, and traveled three and a half days to reach Chicago, the city he fondly called "my western home."

A letter to his mother, dated September 1856, reveals both the maturity of his conversion and his delight with a new environment:

> I reached this far-famed city of the West one week ago tonight. . . . I went into a prayer meeting last night, and as soon as I made myself known, I had friends enough. After meeting they came to me and seemed to be as glad to see me as if I were their earthly brother. God is the same here as He was in Boston, and in Him I can find peace.
>
> I have nothing to write that will interest you unless it is that there is a great revival of religion in this city. I go to meetings every night. Oh, how I do enjoy it! It seems as if God was here Himself. Oh, mother, pray for us. Pray that this work may go on until every knee is bowed. I wish there could be a revival in Northfield, that many might be brought into the fold of Christ.[10]

That letter reflects the heartbeat of a nineteen-year-old convert. A fire had been lighted within that would ultimately ignite the hearts of hundreds of thousands of people around the world. The once shy, embarrassed, country boy would be raised up by God to become *the* evangelist of the nineteenth century.

10. Ibid.

Years later, Moody returned to Boston. He was hounded by the press, and he preached before large crowds. Looking back on his fruitful life, Moody pointed to his encounter with Christ in that old Boston shoe store as the most significant event of his life. For it commenced a life-long ministry, and it opened the door of eternity for his own lost soul.

CHAPTER 2

D. L. Moody's
Early Sunday School

*I am in a hurry tonight and you must excuse
me for not writing more, this time. I am in a hurry.*
—D. L. Moody, in *Moody:*
A Biographical Portrait

D. L. Moody probably had no more than a fifth grade education, and yet he never stopped learning. The Sunday school, more than any other organization, influenced and prepared him for a life of future service. It was through a Sunday school teacher, Edward Kimball, that he experienced conversion to Jesus Christ. It was in the Sunday school of the First Baptist Church that he met his bride-to-be, lovely Emma Revell. It was the Sunday school that nurtured and developed the raw gifts possessed by the dynamic evangelist.

As soon as nineteen-year-old D. L. arrived in Chicago, he identified with the Plymouth Street Congregational Church, where his Uncle Calvin was a member. Anxious to help others, he sought a Sunday school class to teach, only to be denied. It was the custom of the times for those who attended church on a regular basis to rent a pew for family and friends. Enthusiastically, young D. L. rented four pews and then promptly packed them with young people, morning and evening.

Possessing boundless energy, he set aside Sunday afternoons for a little mission Sunday school on the corner of Chicago Avenue and Wells Street, possibly the very corner where Moody Bible Institute's Culbertson Hall is located today. Again, D. L. offered his services to lead a Sunday school class. The superintendent agreed to allow him to lead a class provided he would bring in his own pupils. Moody's son-in-law, A. P. Fitt, writes:

> Next Sunday Moody appeared with eighteen ragged, dirty "hoodlums," gathered off the streets, but each nonetheless needing to be saved. Turning these children over to some of the other teachers, Moody sought out more scholars, until he filled the school to overflowing. He had no idea that he himself could teach, but devoted to God his one talent of being able to "drum up" recruits, both young men and children, for the services of the house of God.[1]

From childhood on, D. L. Moody displayed a concern for the poor and less fortunate. That affinity increasingly characterized his life's work. Not everyone appreciated the appearance and conduct of Moody's newfound friends, however. Some even suggested that it might be better if he started his own Sunday school.

In the fall of 1858 Moody did just that. Along with some business helpers, twenty-one-year-old Moody launched a Sunday school in, of all places, a saloon. Shortly, larger quarters were needed, and with the help of a former mayor, "Long John" Wentworth, Moody and his associates secured the facilities of the North Market Hall for Sunday afternoon. The mayor saw Moody's efforts as a hand of help to the restless and often underprivileged poor of the city.

From the very beginning of his Sunday school work, D. L. Moody showed signs of leadership. Added to his overflowing energy and enthusiasm was his gift for enlisting others to share in the work. Though at times young Moody was crude, he nevertheless knew how to enlist helpers: "Seeking out some of the street arabs

1. A. P. Fitt, *The Life of D. L. Moody* (Chicago: Moody, n.d.), pp. 27-28.

who did not like the Wells Street mission school and had therefore dropped out, Mr. Moody invited them to assist him in his new venture. The boys were pleased to become partners, and willingly entered upon the work. One of those boys subsequently became postmaster of Chicago and the commander-in-chief of the Grand Army of the Republic."[2]

Moody and his helpers would arrive at the hall as early as 6:00 A.M. each Sunday to prepare the auditorium for afternoon Sunday school. They rolled out all that needed to be rolled out. Furniture and chairs were set up and placed in as attractive a setting as possible. Moody looked upon this work as true service to God and just as important as supervising the Sunday school. Though the work was tedious to some, it was an important step in Moody's preparation for arranging halls and auditoriums across the nation and eventually around the world. Often Moody remarked, "I'd rather put ten men to work than do the work of ten men." Moody early on displayed the ability to organize and delegate work.

The Sunday school sessions were never dull. Moody believed it was a sin to be boring. He felt that as the person in charge, he was responsible for the tone and direction of the service. The hour and a half included spirited singing, Scripture reading, prayer, an exciting testimony or illustration, perhaps a contest, and then the lesson time.

Students, with the consent of the Sunday school superintendent, were allowed to audit various classes periodically. This resulted in some teachers—either because of lack of preparation, talent, or inspiration—ending up with no pupils to teach. Nevertheless, in a few short years, D. L. Moody's Sunday school numbered some 1,500 pupils, the largest in the West and perhaps in the entire United States.

2. Ibid, p. 27.

D. L. Moody was a young man in a hurry. To save time he purchased an Indian pony so that he could visit more homes in a day. While he made his Sunday school visits, he allowed the neighborhood children to ride his pony. Picnics excited him and made him a favorite with all ages.

On one occasion Moody promised a new suit of clothes, at Christmas, to thirteen street rebels if they would attend each Sunday. Even their street names were tough—Red Eye, Smikes, Madden the Butcher, Jackey Candles, Giberick, Billy Blucannon, Darby the Cobbler, Butcher Lilroy, Greenhorn, Indian, Black Stovepipe, Old Man, Ragbreeches Cadet—and yet Moody had a marvelous way with them. Only one failed to earn a new suit. A. P. Fitt writes:

> Mr. Moody had them photographed "before" and "after," the pictures being known by the titles "Will it pay?" and "It does pay!" This uniformed group became known as "Moody's bodyguard."
>
> Thirteen years later a friend called at a railway ticket office. The agent asked him to step inside, and said: "You do not seem to know me?"
>
> "No, I have not that pleasure."
>
> "You know 'Moody's bodyguard'?"
>
> "Yes; I have a picture of them in my home."
>
> "Well," said the agent, "when you go home, take a square look at the ugliest of the lot, and you will see your humble servant, now a church member and heir to Mr. Moody in that work."[3]

The Sunday school was D. L. Moody's training ground. Little by little, he improved his public speaking. He especially enjoyed telling Bible stories and soon excelled, unless a minister were present, which often frightened him into incoherency.

3. Ibid, p. 31.

Young Moody's first return visit to Northfield in January of 1860 was a whirlwind of a visit. Uncle Zebulon Allen, Betsy's brother-in-law, seems to have felt the brunt of it. J. C. Pollock quotes Uncle Zebulon:

> "My nephew Dwight is crazy—crazy as a March hare. Came on from Chicago last week for a flying visit. I had not seen him but he drove into my yard this morning. You know how cold it was, and his face was as red as red flannel. Before I could say good morning he shouted, 'Good morning Uncle Zebulon, What are you doing for Christ today?' Of course I was startled and finally managed to say 'Come in Dwight and we will talk it over.' 'No I can't stop, but I want you to think about it,' and he turned the sleigh around and went up the hill like a streak of lightening. I tell you he is crazy."[4]

D. L. Moody was indeed a young man in a hurry, and at times he let his light shine like a blowtorch.

The place of the Sunday school cannot be overstated in the life of D. L. Moody. He credits another Sunday school teacher with his awakening to the worth of a human soul. One of his teachers was terminally ill and deeply concerned for his class of twelve to sixteen slum girls. Not one of them had been led to Christ, and now he had been advised to leave Chicago for a milder climate. Moody was captured by the teacher's compassion and volunteered to accompany the dying teacher to visit each pupil. They visited pupil after pupil, with miraculous success, as each girl professed faith in Christ. Moody was overwhelmed. He had never witnessed such concern and such a response. Moody later said that up to that time he had been "numbers" conscious but henceforth would be "soul" conscious.

4. J. C. Pollock, *Moody: A Biographical Portrait* (New York: Macmillan, 1963), p. 39.

Soon Moody was spending less and less time selling shoes and boots and giving more and more time to sharing the gospel with the needy.

Moody soon moved out of his choice boarding-house and lived in a simple YMCA room. He ate in cheap restaurants and determined to live frugally so that he could give himself more fully to the work of the Lord. His brother-in-law, Fleming H. Revell, wrote in 1917, "Mr. Moody never accepted a salary after he gave up business which I have understood yielded him $5,000. His first year after, his income was $150. A test of real faith."[5]

Moody's Sunday school continued to grow. In 1864 a new building was erected on Illinois Street, between LaSalle and Wells. The building was made as plain as possible so that no one, especially the poor, would feel uncomfortable. A sign was posted at the entrance, "Ever welcome to this house of God are the strangers and the poor."

At about this time it was decided to begin an independent church to meet the needs of the adults as well as the children. Moody served as lay pastor until 1866; then a young man became the pastor, with Moody assuming the title of superintendent.

Providentially, Moody's interdenominational Sunday school experiences were preparing this unordained Christian worker to become a great evangelist. The Sunday school proved to be his training ground.

5. Ibid, p. 37.

Three Cheers for Mother:
Betsy Holton Moody

By the grace of God he was what he was; but his life was largely influenced under God, by his mother. Betsy Holton was born February 5, 1805. She came of old Puritan stock that had settled in Northfield, Massachusetts as early as 1673.
> —Paul Moody and A. P. Fitt,
> *The Shorter Life of*
> *D. L. Moody*

The best thing in the world for a man is to have a good mother and a good wife.
> —D. L. Moody, in
> *Mr. D. L. Moody*
> *at Home*

Late last century, at the close of the Northfield Conference summer school, in Northfield, Massachusetts, D. L. Moody led nearly three hundred young men to the house of his mother. Mrs. Moody, then quite elderly, was confined to bed because of a sprained ankle. Usually, she was up and about, hosting D. L.'s friends or talking with students.

To lift his mother's spirits, Mr. Moody asked the boys, who were standing below her window, to sing for her. Enthusiastically, they broke into a college song, and then "Jesus, Lover of My Soul." After someone offered a prayer for the evangelist's mother, D. L. said to the students, "The best thing in the world for a man is to have a good mother and a good wife, and I propose three cheers for my mother."[1]

The students responded with a rousing cheer for Betsy Holton Moody.

Moody's mother lived to be ninety-one. She died just five years before the death of her famous son.

Mrs. Moody's roots went back to the earliest years of our nation's history. She came from Puritan stock. Her ancestors arrived fourteen years after the landing of the Mayflower. She was raised on a farm that was part of a grant from the Indians to one of her ancestors.

Betsy Moody came from a family of thirteen children. She was the fourth child. Her formal education ended when she was thirteen years old. The rest of her learning came from experience at home.

When she was twenty-three, Betsy married Edwin Moody, a farmer and a bricksman. Little is known about Edwin because he died early, leaving Betsy with seven children and eight months' pregnant with twins. Edwin died heavily in debt. Creditors came like vultures to take everything the Moodys owned—including the kindling wood! Betsy Moody faced a situation not unlike that of some single parents today, where the responsibility falls on the shoulders of the mother.

In speaking of her struggles, she later said, "I knew that God had given those children to me, and that He would be a father to them if I would do a mother's part."[2]

Bravely and persistently, she held them together until they were old enough to care for themselves.

1. T. J. Shanks, *Mr. D. L. Moody at Home* (Chicago and New York: Revell, 1886).
2. D. L. Moody, "Funeral Tribute to Betsy Holton Moody," Moody Archives, p. 3.

D. L. Moody was Betsy's fifth child. Many of his memories of his mother are recorded in the eulogy he gave at her funeral.

He remembered her as an energetic, hardworking woman. Her early experiences, combined with her Puritan heritage, forged in her the lifelong habits of industry, economy, and self-sacrifice. Betsy not only made the children's clothing, but she also wove the cloth and made the yarn out of which they were constructed. And when her children were old enough to work outside the home, she took up the job of milking the cows and doing other farm chores.

Betsy Moody was energetic to the end of her life, doing her own housework and reading several newspapers regularly to keep informed of the events of the day. D. L. probably gained his drive from his energetic mother.

Betsy's thrift continued long after the need existed. D. L. continually sought to make life easier for her, and Betsy sometimes rebelled against the comforts he provided. Once Moody found her drinking tea out of a marmalade jar. To improve the situation, he bought her a set of china, which she stubbornly refused to use. According to Betsy's grandson Paul, "So completely the Puritan was she, and so deep-seated the lifelong habits, that it used to seem to us . . . that she preferred to be uncomfortable and found a degree of virtue in it.[3]

As thrifty as Betsy Moody was, she was still a generous person. If her exterior appeared grim, it had a tender heart. D. L. recalls: "She never turned away any poor from her home. There was one time we got down to less than a loaf of bread. Someone came along hungry, and she says, 'Now children, shall I cut your slices a

3. Paul Moody, *My Father* (Boston: Little, Brown, 1938), p. 74.

little thinner and give some to this person?' And we all voted for her to do it. That is the way she taught us."[4]

Betsy Moody tried to bring up her children with a sense of duty to God and to their neighbors. She had the children baptized in a local Unitarian church (a non-Trinitarian wing of the Congregational church). She read to the family from the Bible every morning. She sent them to Sunday school and church. She insisted that the Sabbath be kept strictly from sundown Saturday until sundown Sunday. And although she shed the Calvinist theology of her forefathers, she did not abandon the strict standards of their Puritan ethics. D. L. remembers that she made her children swear vengeance on whiskey and everything else that was an enemy to a healthy family.

When young D. L. Moody claimed Christ as his Savior in 1855, his mother suspected this newfound enthusiasm. As D. L.'s commitment grew and his ministry expanded, she still rejected what he preached, vowing to be a Unitarian until the day she died.

After returning from his extended campaign in Britain in 1875, Moody headed straight for Northfield. There he took a series of meetings in his home territory. Of course his family came, mostly out of respect for their brother and with some pride in his recent notoriety. But they came intending not to budge from their former convictions. Moody had prayed long and earnestly for the conversion of his family, seemingly to no effect.

Then during one of the final meetings, Moody invited those to rise who wished to acknowledge Jesus Christ as the Son of God and trust Him as Savior. To his shock, his seventy-year-old mother stood to her feet. Moody was so overwhelmed that he could barely ask someone else to lead the others in prayer. On the final

4. D. L. Moody, "Funeral Tribute," Moody Archives, p. 22.

night, his brother Samuel also stood to profess faith in Jesus Christ.

With his mother now wholeheartedly in support of his ministry, Moody reset his sights on Northfield. What was once a cold center of Unitarianism would become a focus of great revival in that part of Massachusetts. Eventually, after Moody returned from his home in Chicago, it became the center of his Northfield schools, as well as the focal point of the Student Volunteer Movement. Betsy's conversion to Christ provided some of the incentive for the new thrust of evangelism.

From that point on, Mr. Moody's relationship with his mother deepened. Now, besides very strong family ties, they shared even deeper bonds in Christ.

D. L. eventually bought property to build upon that which adjoined his mother's land. When he was away from Northfield, he kept in close touch with his mother and sent her daily notes and newspaper clippings of his ministry. She followed each phase of the ministry with earnest prayer. Moody said, "Whenever I wanted real sound counsel, I used to go to my mother."[5]

As Mr. Moody began his own family, he looked to his mother as a symbol of family solidarity to be emulated. He said of her, "In one sense she was wiser than Solomon; she knew how to bring up her children. . . . They all loved their home. She won their hearts."[6]

For all these reasons, D. L. Moody could say to those who attended her memorial service, "We are proud that we had such a mother. We have a wonderful legacy left to us."[7]

5. Ibid, p. 16.
6. Ibid.
7. Ibid, p. 20.

CHAPTER 4

D. L. Moody's Balance Wheel:
Emma Revell Moody

She was his educated adviser in the schools, his confidant and sympathizer in all undertakings. A wife and mother, she was a divinely-appointed balance wheel of his existence.

—Emma Dryer, Letter to
Charles Blanchard,
January 1916

Most early biographies of D. L. Moody say little about the influence of his wife, Emma. In general, people underestimate the influence a wife has on a leader. In our own day, it has taken the press a long time to discover the sway a first lady has over a president.

The influence of Emma Revell Moody on her husband came to light in the biographies of Moody written by his two sons, Will and Paul. Yet there is a reason the secret had been kept so well: that is how Emma wanted it. She was content to serve in the background.

It was a Scotswoman, Mrs. Jane Mackinnon, who best summed up her influence. Observing the Moodys on one of their trips to Scotland, she wrote:

> One day was enough to show what a source of strength and comfort she was to her husband. The more I saw of her, the more convinced I was that a great deal of his usefulness was owing to her, not only in the work she did for him, relieving him of all correspondence, but also from her character. Her independence of thought . . . her calmness, meeting so quietly his impulsiveness, her humility . . . so patient,

quiet, bright, humble; one rarely meets just so many qualities in one woman.[1]

Emma Revell was born in London in 1843. When she was six, her father, ship-builder Fleming Revell, emigrated to the United States and settled in Chicago.

D. L. Moody came to Chicago and entered its bustling business world in 1855. It was three years after his arrival that he showed interest in Emma. In 1860, they were engaged. Then, between engagement and marriage, Moody made his agonizing decision to leave business and preach full time. They married in 1862.

The Moodys were opposites in many ways. He was spontaneous, outspoken, lacking in formal education, and boundless in energy and good health. She was conservative, retiring, a teacher with polished manners, and not strong physically.

Because D. L. and Emma were so different, Moody fondly called her "my balance wheel." Despite being such opposites, they were deeply in love. They not only broke the Victorian stereotype by openly showing affection toward each other, but also enjoyed doing things together. Often they drove off in their buggy to spend a few quiet moments together or for short vacations in their beloved New England. Their love continued to the end.

One reason for their closeness was explained by their younger son, who wrote: "To the day of his death, I believe my father never ceased to wonder at two things—the use God had made of him despite what he considered his handicaps, and the miracle of having won the love of a woman he considered so completely his superior"[2]

1. William R. Moody, *The Life of D. L. Moody* (New York: Macmillan, 1930), p. 82.
2. Paul Moody, *My Father* (Boston: Little, Brown, 1938), p. 52.

Emma's influence went far beyond adding depth and sophistication to D. L.'s life. She was a quality partner.

We can see the quality of Emma's partnership in the way that she managed their home. Emma was in charge of family finances. Whenever Moody left for a trip, she even made sure he had money in his pocket. Emma did all she could to free him from ordinary details so that he could give full attention to his preaching. There also were the regular household chores, such as canning vegetables and preserves from their garden and orchard. And she entertained her husband's many friends who visited Northfield. Sometimes after local meetings, D. L. would bring home groups of twenty and thirty guests.

Having been a teacher, Emma taught herself Latin grammar to help her children with their schoolwork. Especially on Sunday afternoons, she taught them the Scriptures and helped them memorize passages from the psalms and gospels. As their primary teacher, Emma prayed that their children would have "not halfway, but an out-and-out commitment to Christ."

We can also see the quality of Emma's partnership in the way that she involved herself in D. L.'s work. On trips, she shielded him from "interruptions, bores, and cranks—always in abundance." Early in his ministry, she got involved in inquiry room work. Later she focused on other tasks. She became his personal secretary and handled most of his mail. She advised him on his itinerary and at times helped him prepare his addresses.

Emma's contributions even extended to the founding of Moody Bible Institute. Some one-hundred years ago, when the institute was called "The Chicago Evangelization Society," Moody was irritated because of some opposition and bickering from within the Society.

Exasperated, Moody sent a letter of resignation, telling them he was "sick and tired" of the controversy and would expend his energies elsewhere.

It was Emma who wrote a nineteen-page letter to those leading the society, assuring them her husband was merely frustrated and not opposed to the work. And it was Emma who urged him to telegraph a withdrawal of his resignation. Had Emma not intervened, it is possible the misunderstanding would have continued and the entire project would have failed.

Emma Revell Moody was not a wallflower. She was a faithful, hardworking, bright co-laborer in the intercontinental ministry of her husband.

Occasionally at Moody Bible Institute James M. Gray's "Fellowship Song"is sung ("God bless the school that D. L. Moody founded.") Perhaps another stanza should be added: "God bless the school that Emma Moody salvaged."

CHAPTER 5

The Chicago Fire Catastrophe

*This conflagration struck a devastating blow
at Moody's fortunes. His home with his family's
personal belongings, the YMCA's downtown building, and the church that had grown out of his mission Sunday school were all reduced to ashes. The
problems of rebuilding were awesome.*
— James F. Findlay, Jr.,
*Dwight L. Moody,
American Evangelist*

Monday, October 9, 1871, Ira D. Sankey spent most
of the day alone floating in a boat off the shore of Lake
Michigan. It was one of the few safe places to be during
the Great Chicago Fire. His partner, D. L. Moody, had
fled with his family in the night to the western suburbs.

Both men were stunned. Sankey had just left his
home and a secure job in Pennsylvania to join Moody in
his mission work to the people of Chicago.

Everything Moody had worked for was gone. The
fire destroyed all he had built since arriving in Chicago
fifteen years earlier. The fire consumed three and a half
square miles, destroying 1,800 buildings. Property dam-
age was estimated at more than 200 million dollars.
Ninety thousand people were left homeless, and 300
were dead. Robbery, looting, and crime added to the
horror of the catastrophe.

Farwell Hall, the YMCA hall for which Moody had
raised the money, was burned to the ground. More than
the YMCA's flagship building in the United States, it was
also the hub of Moody's ministry. On the night the fire
broke out, Moody preached there to a crowd of some
two thousand people, as he did each Sunday evening.

37

The Illinois Street Church, the outgrowth of Moody's mission Sunday school, was also totally destroyed. With the massive evacuation of Chicago, Moody's workers were scattered so widely that the work had to be completely reorganized.

As with all tragedies, it is baffling to know why things like the Chicago Fire happen. The fire seemed a devastating blow to Moody's work in Chicago, as well as to the families who lost loved ones and all their earthly possessions.

We can never fully answer the question, "Why?" Nevertheless, Christians believe that God is providentially involved in the events of history. And at times we can catch a glimpse into God's plan.

Even a casual study of D. L. Moody's life reveals that this catastrophe marked a turning point in his ministry. Consider some of the changes that took place in Moody's life, partly as a result of the fire.

1. *New outreach in Chicago.* Immediately after the fire, Moody began raising money to rebuild his work. In two and a half months, he built the North Side Tabernacle to accommodate the work of the Illinois Street Church and several city missions that had burned. By night, the tabernacle became a gospel center and a shelter for the homeless. Hundreds were attracted by its bright lights and warmth as they came to hear the gospel. By day, the tabernacle was a center for the distribution of food and clothing.

Suffering, loss, and catastrophe brought new openness to the gospel among the city's peoples. Wave after wave of spiritual revival swept those meetings as people responded to the good news of God's love and grace.

2. *New church.* In a few years the tabernacle gave way to the Chicago Avenue Church. In fact, the *Encyclopaedia Britannica* comments, "The business district was largely rebuilt within a year, and within three there were hardly scars of the calamity. Wood was barred

from a large area (subsequently from the entire city), and a new Chicago of brick and stone, larger, finer and wealthier, had taken the place of the old. Business and population showed no setback in their progress."[1]

3. *New Urgency.* On the night of the fire, Moody preached about the life of Christ. To a packed audience in Farwell Hall he asked, "What will you do with Jesus Christ?" But he told the people to think about it and come back next week to decide. Moody never saw that audience again. Moody said, "That was the worst mistake I ever made."

In retrospect, he said, "I want to tell you of one lesson I learned that night: . . . that is, when I preach, I press Christ upon the people then and there and try to bring them to a decision on the spot."[2]

Whether speaking to one or ten thousand, Moody would discreetly attempt to lead his audience to settle the matter of their eternal destiny. Lovingly, wisely, even quietly, yet definitely, he called for a decision.

4. *New life.* Up until the fire, Moody was overloaded with a multitude of administrative duties. He was torn between the desire to be a spiritual and social organizer for Chicago and the desire to be an evangelist. Moody kept hanging onto his administrative successes. But three days before the Chicago holocaust, Moody wept and prayed, crying out to God for greater service and power in his ministry. He prayed for the fullness of the Holy Spirit in his life and ministry.

That is exactly what he got. With all his efforts burned to a crisp, Moody was thrown back upon the mercy and grace of God. Then in December, on a trip to New York, the double-mindedness and dryness in his life gave way to a flood of refreshment by the Holy Spirit.

1. *Encyclopaedia Britannica,* 11th ed., s.v. "Chicago."
2. William R. Moody, *The Life of D. L. Moody* (New York: Macmillan, 1930), p. 131.

Moody later cited that as the moment when God gave him greater single-mindedness in evangelism, greater power in his preaching, and a greater harvest of souls in his work.

5. *New ministry.* To break free from his Chicago ties, as well as from his administrative duties, Moody accepted a call to preach in England. After his initial relief work in Chicago was over, he set out in 1873 for what became his first great evangelistic campaign in Great Britain.

Unexpected and unplanned as it was, that campaign marked the beginning of his worldwide ministry. Moody stayed in Britain until 1875 and then returned to carry on meetings on the East Coast, where blessings continued to flow. As one Anglican pastor put it, "Moody took the people of Britain in one hand, and America in another, and lifted them up to the glory of God." He became the most noted evangelist on both continents.

Unprecedented ministry, unprecedented conversions, and an outreach that continues to this day: those were the results of the refiner's fire. By the end of his life, Moody could see through the smoke of the Chicago Fire to recognize the other side of catastrophe. Moments of catastrophe often mark the beginning of a brand new day.

CHAPTER 6

D. L. Moody Had A Son

If God will only make our children His own,
faithful and earnest, it is the best that we can ask of
Him for them.

—Emma Moody, in
D. L. Moody,
American Evangelist

In his last letter, the apostle John wrote, "I have no greater joy than to hear that my children walk in truth" (John 1:4).

John was speaking about his children in the faith. Yet his words also express the hopes of Christian parents. They, too, long to see their children walk in God's truth. When our children fall away, we experience great sorrow. This can be doubly true of the children of pastors and missionaries, who live in the public eye.

D. L. and Emma Moody had three children: Emma (born in 1864), Will (born in 1869), and Paul (born in 1879). Of the three, it was Will who gave them the most concern, especially during his high school and college years.

While a student at Moody's own Mount Hermon school, Will wrote to his father, who was traveling, and made clear that he was rebelling against the religion of his parents. He spoke of his "growing dislike of the Bible."[1]

When Will left for studies at Yale, he had little interest in spiritual things and aspired to be a doctor. During those college years, his parents worried a great deal

1. James F. Findlay, Jr., *D. L. Moody, American Evangelist* (U. of Chicago Press, 1969), p. 383.

about him. Though they wanted him to have the advantages of a good education, they feared for his beginning "in college without any reliance on Christ."[2]

Naturally, the Moodys grieved that their older son was defiant toward the faith that was the passion of their lives. The evangelist spoke of this as "the greatest sorrow I have on earth."[3] He wrote to Will and told him plainly: "Sometimes my heart is so heavy and sad to think that you have such contempt for the one that has done so much for your mother and father, all that we are or have has come from Him."[4]

Writing to a friend in England, Will's mother expressed her hope for all her children, saying, "If God will only make our children His own, faithful and earnest, it is the best that we can ask of Him for them."[5]

When things looked grim with Will, Moody blamed himself for his son's spiritual condition. In another letter to Will, he said, "I sometimes think it is my fault, if I had lived more consistently you would not be so disgusted with what is so near to my heart."[6]

While the three children were growing up, the Moodys tried to rear them with a knowledge of Christian truth, but they also tried not to overexpose them to ministry-related activities. They wanted to make Christianity inoffensive to their children. Moody steered away from dull piety. And despite his very public life, he tried to give them a "normal" childhood.

We can see that in the family prayers at breakfast: they never came before the meal. Moody said he was

---

2. J. C. Pollock, *Moody: A Biographical Portrait* (New York: Macmillan, 1939), p. 237.
3. William R. Moody, *The Life of D. L. Moody* (1930), p. 506.
4. Pollock, *Moody,* p. 236.
5. Findlay, *D. L. Moody,* p. 379.
6. Pollock, *Moody,* p. 236.

against "tantalizing a hungry family, by the smell of coffee and bacon while devotions were going on."[7]

Another principle that guided the Moodys was to balance privilege with discipline. On the one hand, Moody wanted his children to have all the benefits he lacked as a boy—education, travel, toys, and hobbies. But on the other hand, he hoped to teach them the discipline of denial. One of his boys recalls his father's ordering them to do the weeding barefoot!

At home, Moody was not "all work and no play." One of his sons described him as "a stout, bearded Peter Pan, a boy who never grew up."[8] They remembered his humor and the games he played with them. They recalled the practical jokes he played on them, such as the time he dropped a squealing piglet through the window of the playroom where young Emma was entertaining her friends.

Will's rebellion took place in this context of a caring, loving home. It would be fruitless to speculate why he rebelled. But it is important to note the limits of his rebellion. It was against a faith, not against the parents he loved.

What did Moody do to win Will back during those years of trial?

One way was to pray for God's help. In a letter to Will, he said, "I have never prayed for you as I do now."[9]

Another was to keep the lines of communication open. It is startling that Will felt free to write to his father and tell him about his rejection of the faith. And we know that, no matter how busy, Moody always took time to write to his children.

7. Pollock, *Moody*, p. 236.
8. Paul Moody, *My Father* (Boston: Little, Brown, 1938), p. 27.
9. Findlay, *D. L. Moody*, p. 380.

Also, Moody was quick to ask for forgiveness if he had been wrong. We see that in his correspondence with Will, and know it was a habit of his life. When Will and Paul were children and did something that evoked their father's temper, they could be sure he would be up in their room apologizing before they went to sleep.

Moody's actions are no sure recipe for bringing a rebellious child back to the Lord. They merely show an example of a father's winning love. His children knew he loved them. And in this way, they learned something of the love of their heavenly Father.

Will Moody eventually was won back. It happened in April 1889. When his father heard the news, he fired off a letter, saying: "I do not think you will ever know until you have a son of your own how much good it did me to hear [this]."[10]

Still later Moody wrote: "I do hope you will lay hold of eternal life with a firm hold. It seems to me it is the only thing worth holding on to in this life. Everything else must pass away."[11]

Will not only took a stand for Christ, but also eventually worked with his father, taking charge of the North-field schools. His father even offered him the post of leading the Chicago school. Will declined that offer, but later became one of the early trustees of the Moody Bible Institute.[12]

10. Findlay, *D. L. Moody,* p 383.
11. Ibid.
12. Ibid.

CHAPTER 7

D. L. Moody, Educator

*My lack of education has always been a great
disadvantage to me; I shall suffer from it as long as
I live.*
—D. L. Moody, in "The Story
of the Northfield Schools"

Rarely does a man with no more than a fifth grade
education become an outstanding educator. But that's
how it was with D. L. Moody. As his son Will commented,
"Moody in his own generation was preeminently known
as an evangelist; in the future he will be known more
and more as an educator."[1]

He could say this because at the end of his father's
life most of his educational projects were just getting un-
derway, and with great promise. Time has proved his
son's prediction to be accurate.

Moody was an educator in many ways. His earliest
efforts in education—as we have shown—involved the
Sunday school. As a boy, even though a Unitarian, he
helped out in some Sunday school visitation.

After his conversion to Christ and move to Chicago,
Moody did the same thing—though more aggressively
—at the Plymouth Street Church, where he rented and
filled pews every Sunday. Later on, he started his own
class.

By 1858, Moody had organized his own mission
school, which grew rapidly. By 1864, the mission school
became the cornerstone of the new Illinois Street Church,

1. William R. Moody, *The Life of D. L. Moody* (New York: Macmillan, 1930), p. 318.

which after his death was named the Moody Memorial Church. The fruit of Moody's Sunday school work still goes on at this significant Chicago church.

A second educational outreach was the Northfield School for Girls (then called the Northfield Seminary), his first official school, founded in 1879. Moody hoped to attract women of "small means and high aims" who wanted a good Christian education.

In 1881, Mr. Moody founded the Mount Hermon School for Boys, a counterpart to the school for girls. At its founding, it was for boys under age sixteen. But in 1885, it was reorganized to train students sixteen and up.

Both the Northfield Seminary and the Mount Hermon School for Boys are still operating. Nestled in beautiful northern Massachusetts near the Connecticut valley, they are known collectively as the Northfield Mount Hermon School. Although the Northfield Mount Hermon School no longer provides an explicitly Christian education, it ranks high among America's prep schools.

The Young Men's Christian Association, which Moody joined in 1854 in Boston, was another project close to his heart. In Chicago, he greatly assisted the city's YMCA. Moody not only raised great sums of money for the association but also served as its international president in 1879.

A fifth educational endeavor was the Northfield Summer Conference, opened in 1880, designed to provide summer Christian training for college students and Christians in general. Moody invited many of the great evangelical preachers and teachers of the day as instructors. In part, the Northfield Summer Conference led to the formation of the Student Volunteer Movement.

The Chicago Evangelistic Society, now known as the Moody Bible Institute, was founded in 1887. The institute not only has continued as an undergraduate school for Christian education but has expanded its work through the addition of new ministries: a book publishing house (1895), a magazine (1900), a correspondence school (1901), an evening school (1903), a radio station (1926), a film company (1945), a missionary aviation school (1946), a broadcasting network (1981), and a graduate school (1985).

In 1895, D. L. Moody founded the Colportage Association, which produced inexpensive Christian literature to be sold by a network of book salesmen, or "colporteurs." Now called Moody Press, it publishes and distributes Christian literature around the world. Mr. Moody also played a part in the early stages of Glasgow Training Institute in Glasgow, Scotland, which continues to this day preparing Christian workers. In light of this barrage of activity, what was it that motivated Moody to give so much of his life to education?

Part of Moody's motivation must have been related to his own lack of formal training. In 1880, he said, "My lack of education has always been a great disadvantage to me; I shall suffer from it as long as I live."[2] Moody wanted others to have what he lacked. He wanted to make Christian education available and affordable.

Also, Moody was burdened to train Christian workers. As he conducted his evangelistic campaigns, he found few Christian workers qualified to counsel in the inquiry room. There was a need for pastors' assistants, city missionaries, and evangelists—people who would stand in the gap between the laity and the clergy. Moody hoped his new schools would teach Christians the basics of Scripture and the Christian life.

Moody was inspired as well by his visits to England. While there, he saw the works of George Mueller and C. H. Spurgeon. Moody returned from Britain overflow-

---

2. "The Story of the Northfield Schools," pamphlet, Northfield Archives.

ing with ideas of what might be done in the United States.

There was also a social and economic motivation. Rapid industrialization and urbanization had brought unrest to American cities. Moody believed that by bringing the gospel and Christian education to the urban poor through his graduates, he could contribute to the peace and order of major American cities like Chicago.

Some have suggested other reasons for Moody's interest in founding schools. One author has offered the view that Moody turned his emphasis from evangelism to education as his evangelistic opportunities waned. But it appears more accurate to see Moody's work in education as a means to evangelize.

From this survey of his work, it becomes clear that Moody's interest in education was lifelong. We see it in his early work with the Sunday school movement and the YMCA.

Furthermore, Moody's interest in education was inseparable from his concern for evangelism. There was a vital connection between his educational ideals and his religious views. As Will Moody has written, everything his father did was related to his Christian faith, which, in turn, found expression in a thousand different ways.

Although there were differences in his schools, they all reflected Moody's interest in practical and explicitly Christian education. The schooling in Northfield was preparatory compared with Chicago's orientation toward direct ministry, but they were both to be strongly related to the Bible.

One of the aims of the Northfield Seminary was to combine general instruction with instruction in the Bible, given in a Christian spirit. According to an early catalog of the school, "the Bible is to have practicality and not only in name, the first place among the textbooks used."[3]

3. "An Early Catalog of the Northfield Seminary," Northfield Archives.

Instruction was to be in things common to all evangelical churches.

What needs to be emphasized is that for D. L. Moody, education was never an end in itself. It was meant to direct individuals to Christ and make them useful for His service. Moody occasionally scorned those who pursued education for education's sake. "An educational rascal," he would say, "is the meanest kind of rascal."

For Moody, education and Christianity went together. The God of Truth, the Truth Incarnate, and especially the Word of Truth—the Bible—was the center of all educational endeavor. Of course, Moody read other books. But he had an important rule, which he hoped would guide his schools: "I do not read any book, unless it will help me to understand *the* Book."[4]

In 2 Timothy, Paul described some well-educated individuals as "ever learning, and never able to come to the knowledge of the truth." That characterizes much of the liberal arts education in America today, which has been severed from its Christian roots.

Moody believed that an alternative course should be pursued. We should be "ever learning" so that we are "ever able" to come to a knowledge of the truth. Truth must have boundaries, or else it will be redefined in the name of some other, lesser truth.

For Moody, those boundaries were determined by his Christian confession and love for God's written Word. These provided both a unifying center and an intense motivation for all his work as an educator.

4. "Moody Quotes," compiled by Northfield Seminary.

CHAPTER 8

D. L. Moody's
Social Conscience

The nation is now crying "Reform!" There will be no true reform until Christ gets into our politics. Men are all naturally bad and cannot reform until the reformer gets into their hearts.

—D. L. Moody, in
Moody: His Words,
Works, and Workers

There was no preacher more practical and civic amongst us.

—Sir George Adam Smith,
speaking of D. L. Moody

Between 1860 and 1914, American society experienced drastic changes. It was an era of urbanization, immigration, and industrialization—movements that magnified the social and spiritual problems of the day.

At the end of the Civil War, America was a rural nation—a gigantic farm. In 1860, only nine cities had a population exceeding 100,000. By 1890, that number had grown to thirty-eight. And by 1920, it was sixty-eight. During those years, 21 million immigrants arrived. The U.S. population exploded from 31 million to 91 million people.

Along with an increase in concentrated population centers came a revolution in American industry. The work force increased by 700 percent, the rate of production by 2,000 percent, and the rate of investment capital by 4,000 percent. Men like Rockefeller, Carnegie, Morgan, and Vanderbilt pushed America into a new age of production. Transport was faster. Factories were newer. Production was mechanized.

The social and spiritual effects of that revolution are still debated. Established communities disintegrated. Man's attachment to the land and rural life was severed. Old ways were forsaken. Dislocated people poured into our cities, where they worked in controlled environments, often for cheap pay.

Responses to the new urban problems varied. The self-help movement had its origin at that time. That age also saw the rise of an army of social reformers. Labor unions were founded. In some churches, a social gospel movement became prominent. Ultimately, it was the era that gave birth to the welfare state.

That was the generation in which D. L. Moody preached.

Moody was not a "social reformer" but an evangelist. He made that clear. In 1877, he said, "The nation is now crying 'Reform!' I don't know how long they are going to continue that cry; they have kept it up ever since I can remember, but there will be no true reform until Christ gets into our politics. Men are all naturally bad and cannot reform until the reformer gets into their hearts."[1]

One reason Moody did not give in to the reform impulse is that he was after a deeper reform. His belief in original sin and human depravity kept him from a mere reformist mindset. The first thing that needed reforming was not the social mechanism, but the internal spring. Moody preached individual reformation through regeneration.

Although as a rule Moody did not belittle social action, his primary interest was the human soul. He believed that changing the structures of society without

1. W. H. Daniels, *Moody: His Words, Works, and Workers* (New York: Nelson and Philips, 1877), pp. 185-86.

addressing the soul was a vain exercise. "Whitewashing the pump," he said, "won't make the water pure."[2]

Another reason Moody avoided supporting the reform efforts of his time is that he believed social evils, which had their origin in individuals, should be dealt with by individuals. He said: "A heart that is right with God and man seldom constitutes a social problem, and by seeking the kingdom of God and His righteousness, nine-tenths of social betterment is effected by the convert himself, and the other tenth by Christian sympathy."[3]

Though it is true that social evil originates in the human heart, Moody overlooked the fact that man-made social structures can be unjust. Overturning them often takes more than conversion and Christian sympathy. So, in one sense, Moody's individualism blinded him to the social and structural dimensions of sin. But in another sense, his individualism was necessary, for the regeneration about which he preached takes place not in mass man but in individual man.

A third reason Moody steered clear of reformers is that most of them happened to be "progressives." They believed in human effort and its ability to usher in the kingdom of God or its secular equivalent. Moody was not so optimistic. He said, "I look upon this world as a wrecked vessel."[4]

For Moody, ultimate reform would have to wait until the coming of Christ. His hope for the world was not the hope of postmillennialism or social Darwinism. His hope rested on a premillennial return of Christ and His earthly reign.

Unfortunately, some people of this persuasion have done what Moody never did. Yes, Moody's pessimism

2. William R. Moody, *The Life of D. L. Moody* (New York: Macmillan, 1930), pp. 181-82.
3. Ibid., p. 170.
4. Daniels, *Moody,* pp. 475-76.

about culture limited the scope of his social action. But he did not throw social action to the wind. To see that, we need only glance at the many social effects of Moody's ministry.

Moody began his gospel work in "the sands," one of the toughest parts of Chicago. He placed a remarkable Sunday school in the midst of neighborhood saloons, gambling establishments, and prostitution posts. Known first as a soul winner, Moody was also recognized for his kindness in distributing coal, food, and clothing to those in need.

Moody's social concern also showed itself in his desire to educate young people. Moody's schools testify to that passion.

As a leader in the YMCA, Moody helped its relief work by soliciting aid for victims of the Chicago cholera epidemic of 1867 and the Chicago Fire of 1871.

Some writers who criticize Moody's lack of social activism fail to realize the social influence he had simply by sticking to evangelism. They forget how morals and manners are affected by the leaven of strong gospel preaching.

Moody's time in Great Britain provides several examples.

To Glasgow, with all that city's social problems, Moody came not as a reformer but as an evangelist. Yet as biographer John Pollock says, in the wake of his meetings "there resulted a surge of activity spiritual and social through channels old and new."[5]

Moody raised money for orphanages. The committee that organized his meetings decided to perpetuate itself with a new name—the Glasgow Evangelistic Association—and to give itself to both evangelism and phi-

5. J. C. Pollock, *Moody: A Biographical Portrait* (New York: Macmillan, 1963), p. 117.

lanthropy. Spin-offs of the work aided the city's orphans, the hungry, and the poor.

The social good that came from Moody's ministry there was so abundant that years later Sir George Adam Smith could say, "There was no preacher more practical and civic amongst us."

Another example is seen in Moody's influence on younger philanthropists of the day. Two men in particular went on to do important service works in Britain.

Wilson Carlile, who assisted Moody's campaigns of 1875, founded The Church Army (the Anglican counterpart to the Salvation Army). We know that besides imitating William Booth, Carlile drew on Moody's advice.

Thomas Barnardo worked to save destitute children from cruelty and neglect by founding foster homes all over Britain. His biographer says that early in Barnardo's career Moody made a deep and lasting impression on his life. Barnardo even copied some of the methods Moody used in his Chicago work. When Moody wrote about the lives of the twelve most useful men he had known, he called Barnardo "a prince among benefactors" and listed him as his first choice.[6]

One final instance of Moody's influence is found in the Christian Labor Movement of Britain. This was led by progressive evangelicals, along with leading socialists of the day. Kathleen Heasman in her study of evangelical social work in Victorian England, *Evangelicals in Action,* shows how the origin of that movement can be traced in part to the results of the Moody campaigns in the 1870s. The movement was a seedbed for some of the future leaders of the British Labor party, including that party's founder, Keir Hardie.

The point that must be made in all this is that, though Moody was not a social reformer, he had a great

6. Gillian Wagner, *Barnardo* (London: Weidenfeld and Nicholson, 1979), p. 43.

influence on society and the alleviation of its ills. Moody didn't have to join the pack of reformists to do this. He just preached the Word, and when people responded he encouraged them to attempt something great for God.

Moody often repeated the text "To every man his work" (Mark 13:34). Moody's work was to preach the gospel to crowds of people. But he fully recognized that God was raising up others to different forms of service. Those men and women extended Moody's influence in society beyond anything he had ever dreamed.

CHAPTER 9

D. L. Moody and the Student Volunteer Movement

1886-1936 Mount Hermon. Here, in July, 1886, to the glory of God and to the advancement of his kingdom, Dwight L. Moody and the Intercollegiate Young Men's Christian Association of the United States and Canada called together a conference of students from twenty-seven states and many lands beyond the seas. From the spiritual impulse here given, one hundred men offered their lives for foreign missionary service. A work of spiritual awakening was begun in the colleges. Similar conferences were established throughout the world. The Student Volunteer Movement was founded in 1888, and guidance was given the Christian Student movement through the years. "I am the way, the truth, and the life."

—Inscription on a monument
in Northfield, Massachusetts

The nineteenth century is known in church history as the missionary century. The revival in Great Britain, sparked by Wesley's preaching, resulted in a host of new mission societies. The century abounded with British missionary heroes. William Carey and Henry Martyn served in India. David Livingstone was making inroads into Africa. And J. Hudson Taylor began the China Inland Mission.

The American Adoniram Judson was in Burma. However, as the century progressed, American Protestants were distracted by slavery issues, the War Between the States, and denominational struggles. What outreach took place was directed at new settlements in the West and at the immigrants pouring in from Europe. As a result, not many missionaries were sent overseas.

But the situation has changed significantly over the years. Whereas only a few hundred American missionaries were serving abroad in the 1870s, by the 1890s the number had grown to 900. In 1900 it jumped to 5,000. By 1915 it was 10,000. And that number has been growing ever since.

More than any other factor, the Student Volunteer Movement, begun in 1886, accounted for that sudden increase in American participation in foreign missions. The movement aggressively sought to recruit students for world evangelization.

Several streams came together to create a student awakening. One stream was the outgrowth of the "haystack prayer meeting" that took place in 1806 at Williams College. There, Samuel J. Mills and others formed the Society for the Brethren—a student group committed to world evangelization.

Another stream was the outgrowth of the Young Men's Christian Movement, especially its intercollegiate associations. Under the direction of Luther Wishard, those collegiate chapters, meeting at the nation's finest universities and colleges, grew in missionary interest. Wishard confronted D. L. Moody, also a leader in the YMCA, about the need for the student associations of the YMCA to join in an annual conference, perhaps at Moody's school in Northfield.

A third stream was the outgrowth of the work of the Princeton Foreign Missionary Society under the leadership of Robert Wilder. That university group became a driving force behind the Student Volunteer Movement. Its members offered themselves as "willing and desirous, God permitting, to go to unevangelized portions of the world."

A fourth stream was the outgrowth of the work of the "Cambridge Seven" in England. Moody's preaching in the British Isles in the 1870s had resulted in a revival among students at Cambridge and Oxford. Two of the converts from Cambridge were C. T. Studd and Stanley Smith, both prominent athletes who, with five others, joined to form the Cambridge Missionary Seven.

Largely influenced by Moody's preaching, these athletes decided to go to China as missionaries. Their decision received national attention and brought them a wide following as they began to speak for the missionary cause at other British colleges.

In 1886, Wishard convinced D. L. Moody to hold a summer conference for college students at the Mount Hermon School. Moody was reluctant because he believed that only those with great intellectual ability could reach college students.

Wishard persisted, explaining to Moody that the evangelist underrated himself. His direct, forceful appeals inspired college men and aroused in them a love for Christ and the Bible. Moody finally yielded to Wishard's request.

That summer, 250 students from eighty-six colleges gathered at Mount Hermon for a month of Bible teaching and fellowship. Wishard's goal was that the conference would help train students in their faith and bring a cohesiveness to a growing intercollegiate Christian movement.

Attending that conference were delegates from England, a group of students from Princeton led by Wilder, and a group from Cornell, including the newly converted John R. Mott.

Although the Mount Hermon conference did not set out to be a missionary conference, Wilder's passion prevailed. He asked Moody if he could have an evening when the delegates from other nations could present the needs of their own people. That meeting, held July 23, was called "the meeting of ten nations."

It changed the whole tone of the conference, as students came under the power of God's Spirit. They asked for more missionary addresses. A. T. Pierson and others then spoke to the students about the worldwide challenge. By the end of the conference, 100 students had signed a declaration of willingness to serve Jesus Christ in foreign missions. Their watchword was "The Evangelization of the World in This Generation." They became known as the "Mount Hermon One Hundred."

Following the example of the Cambridge Seven, students were chosen to enlist others at colleges across America. Wilder and a small team visited 162 institutions in eight months. Those who returned to full-time studies worked their colleges from within. By the end of that first year, more than 2,000 American students, including 500 women, had affirmed the Mount Hermon declaration.

In time, Mott and Wilder were chosen as members of the Student Volunteer Movement's executive committee. Their passion continued to attract great enthusiasm, especially from 1890 to 1917, the movement's peak years. As chairman, Mott presided over large "quadrennials"—international student missionary conventions held every four years.

Across America, the movement helped prompt an interdenominational student awakening. With it came a great revival of missionary interest. Some actually went overseas; others felt compelled to support missions with their prayers and gifts. The movement's call for absolute consecration to the Great Commission became a heroic endeavor for these young people.

The results of that challenge spilled over into other nations as well. The American Student Volunteer Movement sparked movements throughout Europe. It also inspired countless conferences and conventions in which students came to understand the enormity of the missionary task in a new way. The gathering of "missionary intelligence" was just beginning.

Though the total number of Student Volunteer Movement missionaries is difficult to estimate, historian Earle Cairns has observed that "by 1945 it had recruited 20,500 missionaries."[1] Independent and denominational mission societies benefited greatly from that influx of manpower.

Many offshoots grew from the Student Volunteer Movement. Among those offshoots were the Student Christian Movement, the World Student Christian Federation, and, later, the InterVarsity Christian Fellowship. Mott emerged as the great missionary statesman of the Western church, ultimately winning a Nobel Peace Prize in 1946. Biographer John Pollock and others cite the Ecumenical Movement as being another offshoot of the Student Volunteer Movement. In its earliest form the Ecumenical Movement was a child of the International Edinburgh Missionary Conference chaired by Mott in 1910, though in its later form it gave birth to the World Council of Churches (1948).

The Student Volunteer Movement is worthy of study by evangelicals. Not only does it show the passion of missionary-minded people, but it also illustrates how a movement can broaden and lose its original vision.

Whatever the loss of original vision, it is clear that at its inception D. L. Moody was a great inspiration to the movement. We see it in his work with the YMCA, in his evangelistic campaigns in Scotland and England, and especially in his work in the convening of the 1886 Mount Hermon conference.

Moody did not attempt to lead the Student Volunteer Movement. He would often say, "It's my job to get

1. Earle Cairns, *Christianity Through the Centuries* (Grand Rapids: Zondervan, 1981), p. 427.

things going." As Pollock notes, "His genius had touched into life a latent movement which other men could carry forward."[2]

In 1928, Mott himself said, "I sat at [Moody's] feet at the first intercollegiate Christian conference held at Mount Hermon in 1886, and from that time to this, the evangelistic impulse he imparted has never lost its power, nor have I ceased to give, as he did, right of way to evangelism."[3]

2. J. C. Pollock, *Moody: A Biographical Portrait* (New York: Macmillan, 1963), p. 225.
3. *John R. Mott, Addresses and Papers* (New York Associated Press, 1946-1947), 4:996.

CHAPTER 10

The Birth of
Moody Bible Institute

*Organization was not preeminently Mr. Moody's
endowment. Founding, evangelizing and quick execution were emphatically his. . . . He was, like
Elijah, a divinely equipped "flying artillery" on
life's battlefield. He broke the enemy's centers and
in so doing, incidentally aroused new organizers
and was an inspiration to their constructive work.*
—Emma Dryer, Letter from Emma Dryer
to Charles Blanchard, January 1916

A considerable amount has been written about the
founding of the Moody Bible Institute of Chicago. Robert
Flood and Jerry Jenkins have given a popular account in
the centenary volume, *Teaching the Word, Reaching the
World* (Chicago: Moody, 1985), pp.38-45. A more in-
depth study is offered in Gene Getz's work, *MBI: The Story
of the Moody Bible Institute* (Chicago: Moody, 1969),
pp. 21-59.

Still other accounts can be found in such biogra-
phies as *Moody,* by J. C. Pollock (London: Hodder and
Stoughton, 1963), *Dwight L. Moody, American Evange-
list 1837-1899,* by James F. Findlay, Jr. (Chicago: U. of
Chicago Press, 1969; pp. 321-38). Another helpful but
less well-known source is a letter Emma Dryer wrote in
January of 1916 to Charles Blanchard, then president of
Wheaton College in Wheaton, Illinois (Moody Archives).

There is little need to repeat what has already been
written or is still in print. If the reader is interested in a
chronological sequence, he should review the books
mentioned. What might be more useful in this study is

to survey some of the prominent factors that led to the initial founding of the Chicago Evangelization Society in February 1887.

Institutional histories often fall into one of two categories. Some are people-centered, focusing exclusively on the strong personalities behind a movement. For example, *Teaching the Word, Reaching the World* tells the story of the founding of Moody Bible Institute primarily through a discussion of the lives of D. L. Moody and the three women who labored with him, Emma Dryer, Nettie McCormick, and Emma Moody.

In the other category are the histories that tend to emphasize environmental factors. Various doctoral theses on Moody's life follow this pattern, presenting Moody as a product of his age. Thus, though he does not exclude other explanations, Findlay sees unrest among the working people of Chicago as a major catalyst in the founding of the Moody Bible Institute.

But the careful observer who stops to look at the history of any significant institution or event will discern both human as well as environmental factors working together in God's providence. For instance, when historians reflect upon the political rise of the religious right in America in the 1980s, they will learn most if they consider not only personalities, such as Jerry Falwell, but also prevailing conditions, such as the secularization of American life during the close of the twentieth century.

What were some of the factors that led to the founding of the Moody Bible Institute? There were at least four, two having to do with personalities and two having to do with environment.

The first of those personalities was D. L. Moody himself. The Chicago school probably would not have come into existence apart from D. L. Moody's own towering personality and vision.

Early in his career, through his work in the Sunday School and the YMCA, Moody came to love the people of Chicago. Out of a deep concern to see men and women brought to a saving relationship with Christ, he gave himself to urban evangelization. When the Great Fire of 1871 destroyed his base of operations, he immediately set out to rebuild his work.

But even before the fire, Moody sensed that the needs of the working class and the poor were not being met by American churches. Moody himself was dreaming of an army of middlemen to stand in the gap between the clergy and the common people. His vision was to fill Chicago with Christian workers who would launch out from various mission stations to visit, assist, teach, and distribute literature and to help in campaigns like his own. That vision was clearly articulated much later, in 1886, at Farwell Hall in a meeting with key Chicago evangelical and business leaders to consider urban evangelism.

There Moody said, "I believe we have got to have gap men—men to stand between laity and the ministers; men who are trained to do city mission work. . . . We need the men that have the most character to go into the shops and meet these hard-hearted infidels and skeptics. They have got to know the people and what we want is men who know that, and go right into the shop and talk to men. Never mind the Greek and Hebrew, give them plain English and good Scripture."[1]

So the vision Moody presented that day in Chicago was not a new one for him but was one that had been in his thinking for some time. In fact, it appears to have been at one time the vision he had had for East Northfield, Massachusetts. But as Findlay observes, "Over the years the founder's vision of the Northfield schools as

1. *Chicago Tribune,* January 23, 1886.

training centers in practical evangelization seemed increasingly further from realization."[2]

The problem appears to have been that at the Northfield schools Moody failed to work out a specific program of studies to implement his idea. As a consequence, even early on, the schools began to look a lot like other East Coast academies. But at the second opportunity to organize a school, the opportunity present in Chicago, Moody could remedy that defect, and his vision of "gap men" resurfaced.

The second personality associated with the founding of Moody Bible Institute was Emma Dryer. If D. L. Moody was the visionary behind the idea of the Chicago school, then Emma Dryer was its driving force. Speaking of D. L. Moody years later, Dryer said, "Organization was not preeminently Mr. Moody's endowment. Founding, evangelizing and quick execution were emphatically his. . . . He was, like Elijah, a divinely equipped 'flying artillery' on life's battlefield. He broke the enemy's centers and in so doing, incidentally aroused new organizers and was an inspiration to their constructive work."[3]

In contrast to Moody, Emma Dryer was both a plodder and an organizer. Moody met Emma Dryer in 1870. She was a principal and teacher at Illinois State Normal University. Visiting Chicago in 1871, Dryer responded to the Great Fire and its terrible wreckage by giving herself to relief work alongside D. L. Moody. Observing her work, Moody was favorably impressed. Not wanting to lose such a valuable worker, he tried to persuade her to join his church and utilize her teaching talent for the work of the ministry.

2. James F. Findlay, Jr., *Dwight L. Moody: American Evangelist, 1837-1899* (Chicago: U. of Chicago Press, 1969), p. 320.
3. Letter from Emma Dryer to Charles Blanchard, January 1916, Moody Archives, p. 25.

When Moody first spoke to Emma Dryer about a new training school in Chicago, he appeared to have only women in mind. Men, he thought, could train at the seminaries. Besides, were his school to train the men, the seminaries would probably take offense. Emma Dryer disagreed with Moody and challenged him to enlarge his vision. The need for men and women workers was equally great.

After much soul-searching, Emma Dryer realized that Chicago was where she should stay. Catching Moody's vision for a new work, and convinced that she could make a valuable contribution, she united with Moody's church. It seemed much could be done quickly. Besides, she had Moody's promise that upon his return from Britain he would make the school in Chicago his first work. Unknown to both of them was the fact that Moody would be preoccupied with other things for the next ten years.

Despite Moody's long absence, Dryer initiated a program of Bible work through the church in 1873. Essentially, the program was a school within the church, devoted to personal evangelism among the poor, house-to-house visitation, women's prayer meetings, tract distribution, sewing schools, and so on. This work, most historians agree, was really the seedbed of the Moody Bible Institute. Dryer called it "a child of Moody Church."[4]

The program initiated by Emma Dryer continued for ten years without Moody's active involvement. True, he offered advice and money, along with his best wishes. But he still had not come through on his promise to make it his first work.

During that time Dryer enlisted outside help, and the ministry grew. Among those who supported her was

4. Ibid., p. 28.

Nettie McCormick, wife of the prominent Chicago industrialist Cyrus McCormick, Jr.

By 1884, Dryer had added a second facet to her existing work and initiated a May Institute. The May Institute was a short-term Bible institute program designed to offer a more intensive curriculum than the Bible work provided. The May Institutes became a testing ground for a more permanent year-round work. They were held each year until 1889, when the full year curriculum of the Chicago Evangelistic Society was finally set in place.

To limit the study of the origins of the Moody Bible Institute to these two people—Moody the visionary and Dryer the organizer—gives only part of the story. Moody and Dryer lived in environments that both shaped and made way for them.

One of those environmental factors, and one that is sometimes forgotten, though it is visible in the records, is the influence of British evangelicalism on both Moody and Dryer. In the late nineteenth century, Britain was at its peak as a world power. The military and economic might of the British Empire was great. So was the influence of its church life. There was a significant evangelical movement in Britain at this time. It included a network of ministries that broke through state church barriers and included non-conformist churches. That can be seen most clearly in the area of missionary outreach, in which British Christians were at the forefront.

In reviewing the events of Moody's life, one sees the British Isles pulling him to their shores like a magnet. Moody made several trips to Britain, and most of them took place before his Chicago school was founded. He went in 1867, in 1870, and in 1872. His first great evangelistic campaign there lasted from 1873 to 1875. He made two visits in the 1880s for another campaign: 1881-1883 and 1883-1884. And then there was his final visit in 1891-1892.

The reasons Moody gave for returning so often to Great Britain included the following: "To learn more Bible at the feet of English Bible students," "to look for something to take back," and "to sample a wide variety of things."

What was the evangelist sampling? It seems that Moody was taking notes from the various evangelical ministries of the day and "nicking" ideas for the work God had given him in his homeland.

For example, in his early trips Moody made it a point to meet and study his hero C. H. Spurgeon at the Metropolitan Tabernacle in London. While in London, he visited some of the spin-off ministries of Spurgeon's church. He also met with George Mueller and carefully observed his orphanage work. Because of his involvement with the YMCA, Moody wanted to meet with that movement's founder, George Williams. He was impressed with the mother organization's evangelical methods, such as their evening training school for laymen, and he desired to see this kind of outreach in cities like Chicago.

Another influence on Moody at this time was the Rev. William Pennefather, Rector of St. Jude's, Mildmay Park, London. In 1856, Pennefather established a ministry that consisted of a conference hall for missionary and evangelistic enterprises, along with a deaconess house to train women workers. In Moody's early conversations about a Chicago work, the British operation in Mildmay was his ideal of what should be done.

In Emma Dryer's account of the origins of the Chicago schools, she recalls that "Mr. Moody wished me to visit the Mildmay and other institutions, with reference to the contemplated work in Chicago."[5] So from 1879 to 1880, Emma Dryer herself went to England to sample

5. Ibid., p. 17.

what Moody had been fired up about. She lived in the Mildmay deaconess house for many weeks and then observed other prominent ministries from which she could glean ideas and methods for Chicago.

Beyond the influence of Spurgeon and Pennefather, one other British ministry is likely to have affected Moody's thinking. Moody visited the East London Institute for Home and Foreign Missions, founded in 1872, under the direction of H. Grattan Guiness. This training school was, in a way, a precursor to the American Bible Institute. Guiness's school was one of the institutions that inspired A. B. Simpson to found the Nyack Missionary School in 1882 (the first Bible Institute in America).

It is of interest that Dryer speaks of prayer meetings in 1883 and 1884 that were held in the Bible work room of Chicago's Farwell Hall. The special object of the prayer meetings was the establishment of a greater Bible work in Chicago and the training of home and foreign missionaries. Dryer said, "Our discussions and prayers contemplated something like the Mildmay Deaconess work for women, and the Grattan Guiness's East London Institute for the education of men."[6]

In a footnote to *MBI: The Story of The Moody Bible Institute*, Gene Getz considers the extent to which the Chicago school patterned itself after Guiness's Institute. For the complete, original name of the Chicago work was "The Bible Institute for Home and Foreign Missions of The Chicago Evangelistic Society," strikingly similar to the full name of Guiness's work.[7]

At least one other factor played a significant part in establishing Moody's training school. It was the urban social unrest that Chicago experienced, particularly in 1885 and 1886.

6. Ibid., p. 22.
7. Gene Getz, *MBI: The Story of The Moody Bible Institute* (Chicago: Moody, 1969), p. 23.

Moody knew well the social problems of big city life, as a consequence of his work with young people from the roughest parts of the city. It was his burning conviction that if people of that sector were not evangelized they would be a constant burden. He referred to them as "the neglected masses."[8]

It wasn't just Moody who felt that way. Cyrus H. McCormick, Jr. himself reflected that "the best way to cope with the problem of the poor and labor difficulties was to help Mr. Moody start the Bible school he had in mind, and send workers throughout the city."[9]

The 1870s were a time of financial depression in Chicago. Hard times caused distress among the working people. And the situation was taken advantage of by a small number of agitators who espoused anarchist and Marxist views. Chicago's large immigrant population was somewhat attentive to their petitions. From 1881 to 1884 there appears to have been a brief release from the depression. But then again, in 1884 and in 1885, things turned bad. Workers were laid off, salaries were lowered, and strikes were common. It seems that labor unrest was most intense at the Pullman Palace Car Company and at Cyrus McCormick's harvester works.

In 1885, in the midst of these unsettled conditions, T. W. Harvey presided over a first meeting at Farwell Hall to discuss city evangelism. Moody was there, and he urged those present that if they wanted a school to train workers, they had to raise a quarter of a million dollars before he'd throw his hat in the ring. Moody left the meeting discouraged about the school's future. Privately he confided to Miss Dryer that New York might be a better place for a school.

8. Letter from John Farwell to Nettie McCormick, November 23, 1888, The Nettie McCormick Collection.
9. "Reminiscences of D. L. Moody," by Emma Dryer, Moody Archives.

In January 1886 another meeting was held in Farwell Hall for the purpose of organizing a school in Chicago, the meeting referred to earlier in this chapter. By that time about half the money needed to begin the school had been raised. Sensing that the rest would come and that the time was ripe for evangelical action, Moody made his famous plea for "gap men." The urgency in his voice probably struck a resonant chord with anxious businessmen. Moody said, "Either these people [evidently a reference to those who were causing some of the labor disturbances] are to be evangelized or the leaven of communism and infidelity will assume such enormous proportions that it will break out in a reign of terror such as this country has never known . . . you can hear the muttering of the coming convulsion even now, if you open your ears and eyes."[10]

Though something less than a "reign of terror," the convulsion came in May of that year in the form of the famous Haymarket riot. Evidently those disturbances aided Moody's fund-raising efforts, for the rest of the money needed to launch the school was committed about that time.

On May 3, 1886, a demonstration was held against the McCormick works, where there occurred a lockout of union members. When police tried to disperse the crowd, a bloody clash took place. On May 4, a group of socialist union leaders held a protest at Haymarket Square attended by about a thousand people. Again police tried to disperse the crowd. Someone threw a bomb. Several policemen were killed and pandemonium broke loose.[11]

It is noteworthy that sometime after the clash, Moody trustee and businessman T. W. Harvey wrote a

10. Findlay, *Dwight L. Moody*, p. 327.
11. Tamara K. Hareven, ed., *Anonymous Americans* (Englewood Cliffs, N.J.: Prentice Hall, 1971), p. 284.

letter to McCormick's wife saying that "the only way to convert this dangerous element into peaceful, helpful citizens [is] through the transforming power of Christ." He then went on to say that when Mr. Moody made his appeal to reach those people, his efforts were cordially received.[12]

What seems to have happened is that the social unrest of the time quickened the conscience of a number of affluent Christians, who believed that something urgent had to be done. At that precise moment, Dwight Moody and Emma Dryer came forward with a concrete proposal that had been evolving over the past ten years.

This convergence of people and events led up to the meeting on February 5, 1887, at the Grand Pacific Hotel, where a constitution for the Chicago Evangelization Society was presented and adopted, resulting in the birth of the Moody Bible Institute.

12. Letter from T. W. Harvey to Nettie McCormick, November 16, 1888, The Nettie McCormick Collection.

CHAPTER 11

The Original Trustees of Moody Bible Institute

When Moody organized the Chicago Evangeliza-tion Society in 1886-87, the six members of the board were well known not only in Chicago but all over the world for their great business enterprises and financial sagacity.

—Gene Getz, *MBI: The Story of Moody Bible Institute*

In *MBI: The Story of Moody Bible Institute,* Gene Getz lists several reasons for the institute's quick rise to fame in the late nineteenth century. Along with divine blessing and the school's strategic location, urgent and practical objectives, interdenominational nature, innovative leadership, and famous founder, Getz points to the influence of D. L. Moody's friends in the business world.

Moody, a former businessman himself, had much in common with those men. And he was convinced that Christian businessmen could make a unique contribution to the work of the church.

Today some churchmen speak as if the world of business is wholly corrupt. They appear to want the donations of business but frown on the mechanism of the marketplace. Moody, however, believed in the private stewardship of wealth, and he challenged those in business to use their financial and managerial skills for the glory of God.

We can see the results of Moody's challenge as we review the lives of the first trustees of the new Chicago

Evangelization Society, which would become the Moody Bible Institute. They were among Chicago's movers and shakers, and some had risen to national prominence.

Most had been associated with Moody in the Young Men's Christian Association in the 1860s. As supporters of Moody's evangelistic work, they wanted him to do something in Chicago of a more permanent nature.

Who were the early trustees who laid the foundations of the Moody Bible Institute?

First there was *Nathaniel S. Bouton* (1828-1908), a Presbyterian, who served as a trustee from 1887 to 1890. He was an early contributor to the Bible work of Emma Dryer.

Coming to Chicago in 1852, Bouton bought an architectural iron and railway casting company, which he reorganized as The Union Foundry Works. Because Chicago was central for the railway industry, Bouton was prominent in his field.

But Bouton exercised his influence in other areas as well. In 1857, the mayor of Chicago named him superintendent of Public Works—a job in which he was the first to have Chicago's streets paved. Bouton also served as president of the YMCA and the Chicago Bible Society.

When D. L. Moody sent his resignation to the Chicago Evangelization Society, it was Bouton who protested: "It can not be, Mr. Moody. You must not take this step." In a letter, Bouton urged him, "Remain in your post as long as you live." Bouton foresaw the Chicago work as becoming "very great and prominent."[1]

John V. Farwell (1825-1908). Farwell, a Methodist, arrived in Chicago in 1845 on a wagon of wheat with only $3.75. Yet he rose to prominence both in local business and in national politics.

1. Letter from Nathaniel Bouton to D. L. Moody, Moody Archives.

In business he had an early role in what are still two of Chicago's largest stores. Farwell hired department store founder Marshall Field to his dry goods firm in 1856. The two worked closely together and, in 1866, called themselves Farwell, Field & Co. When the partners split up, there were two firms, the John V. Farwell Co. and the Marshall Field Co. In 1925, Farwell's business was bought by Carson, Pirie, Scott & Co.

Farwell also served as vice president of the Chicago Board of Trade. In politics he was a presidential elector on the Lincoln ticket in 1860. Farwell brought Lincoln to visit Moody's Sunday school early in Moody's ministry. Under President Grant, Farwell was appointed Indian commissioner.

John Farwell became one of Moody's closest friends. In 1859, Moody persuaded him to serve as superintendent of his Sunday school. When Moody's ministry widened, Farwell underwrote many of his expenses and even bought him a house. Eventually, Farwell served as a trustee for the Bible institute from 1887 to 1908.

Farwell's daughter observed that her father had a love for Moody similar to that which existed "only between David and Jonathan."[2]

T. W. Harvey (1835-1909). Harvey had close ties with the Methodist Episcopal church. He served as a trustee from 1887 to 1893.

In Harvey's obituary the *Chicago Tribune* described him as "one of Chicago's pioneer lumbermen, and at one time, the greatest retail lumber dealer in the world."

Harvey came to Chicago with virtually nothing. He started out as a carpenter and eventually bought his own lumber business. Harvey anticipated a sharp increase in

2. James F. Findlay, Jr., *Dwight L. Moody, American Evangelist* (Chicago: U. of Chicago Press, 1969), p. 80.

lumber demand and prices because of a spate of forest fires and the tragic Chicago Fire in 1871. He quietly bought up all the lumber he could. Fortune followed. Harvey turned the lumber industry around in 1878 when he began using railroads to transport logs to the mills.

He not only founded a town (Harvey, Illinois) but also built thousands of houses following the Chicago Fire. He even oversaw the erection of the original Moody Church building.

Harvey served as vice president of the Bible institute and was Moody's adviser on society matters.

Another trustee was *Elbridge G. Keith* (1840-1905). Keith, who came from a Reformed Episcopal church background, served as a trustee from 1887 to 1905.

He came to Chicago in 1857 and rose to become a financier, merchant, and banker. In 1884, Keith served as president of the Metropolitan Bank of Chicago and president of the Chicago Title and Trust Co. He was active in leading the Chicago Board of Education, the YMCA, and the Chicago Bible Society. With his financial background, Keith became D. L. Moody's first treasurer.

A fifth trustee was *Robert S. Scott* (1838-1904). Scott, a Presbyterian, came to Illinois from Ireland in 1856. Starting as a salesman in a dry goods firm, he later joined in a partnership with Carson Pirie & Co., giving the department store its present name. At the time of his death, Scott was the senior partner. He served as a Moody trustee from 1887 to 1900.

Finally, there was *Cyrus H. McCormick, Jr.* (1859-1936). Like his inventor father, Cyrus McCormick, Jr., was a friend and supporter of D. L. Moody. He served on the board of trustees from 1887 to 1893.

In business, McCormick headed the International Harvester Company for thirty-three years. Recognized as one of the wealthiest men in the nation, he was a generous benefactor. A seminary in Chicago is named in his honor.

McCormick's wife was also influential in the founding of Moody Bible Institute.

Each of these trustees was an outstanding Christian businessman. They knew that the gospel must be preached and that this would bring not only salvation but also an internal reform with consequences that social reformers dreamed of but could not achieve.

But they did more than just promote evangelism. They gave to other worthy causes, such as relief for victims of the Chicago Fire and educational ventures throughout the city.

They also gave of their time. Most were involved in directing institutions such as the Chicago Bible Society and the YMCA in addition to the Bible institute. Their giving was not detached for the sake of a tax write-off.

Several of these men had come to Chicago poor. By a combination of drive, ingenuity, and providence, they acquired a great deal of money.

Nevertheless, despite their national prominence, their investments were not limited to temporal things. They saw the importance of investments that reap eternal rewards in the kingdom of heaven.

D. L. Moody may have lacked formal education, but he had business know-how from his early life that never left him. The business elite of Chicago were attracted both to Moody and to his cause.

In turn, Moody put them to work in positions where they could do more good. Although some of their business empires have since disappeared, one of their part-time projects remains strong. It has been more than one hundred years now, and the Bible institute still thrives.

CHAPTER 12

D. L. Moody and Premillennialism

The trump of God may be sounded, for any-thing we know, before I finish this sermon . . . .
—D. L. Moody, "The Return of Our Lord"

Until the mid-1800s, most American evangelicals were postmillennialists. From the colonial period on, Protestants in general believed that the millennial reign of Christ on earth (for 1,000 years, as cited in Revelation 20) would come about through the victorious efforts of Christians on the earth. The actual return of Christ would take place at the end of that period.

It has often been remarked that this prophetic view of things was well suited to the optimistic faith of a young, vibrant nation. Events seemed to verify that things were getting better. And Christianity would be the faith that would cure the ills of society and win the world.

Not until the War Between the States did this view of history and prophecy begin to lose ground. Its chief competitor—premillennialism—held that the present age would grow more corrupt. Its decay could only be reversed by the return of Jesus Christ. The Lord Himself would have to usher in the millennial age. His return would be before the 1,000-year reign and therefore is called premillennial.

Moody, like many of his day, changed his views about future events in the middle of the century. As he recalled in a sermon, "I used to say, '[Christ] can't come in my day. Don't you know that there is to be one thousand years of millennium; that righteousness must increase and wickedness must decrease before he comes?' Ah, my friends, but since I have got a little better acquainted with the Word of God, I find that this is not God's plan."[1]

Moody had certainly embraced a premillennial perspective by the 1870s. Exactly when he changed from the postmillennial outlook of his congregational past is a question of debate. Some argue for a date in the mid-1870s. More likely, the shift came earlier, in the late 1860s.

Emma Dryer, Moody's colleague in Chicago, has written of her first meeting with Moody in the summer of 1870. She recounts, "He surprised me, by abruptly asking, 'Do you understand the doctrine of the coming and Kingdom of Christ?' " to which she responded in the affirmative. Moody then replied, "Why, it is the key to Scriptures!"[2]

It seems that his new found insight came largely from the influence of British Christians who were Plymouth Brethren. Some of them, such as Henry Moorehouse, had visited his home in the late 1860s. In 1867, Moody made one of his early trips to England, partly to learn all he could from the Brethren and their teachings of the prophetic Scriptures.

What is significant about D. L. Moody and premillennialism is that Moody was the first renowned evangelist in America to adopt the premillennial position. His views marked a departure for evangelists and a generation of evangelicals who were influenced by their preaching.

Prophetic truth became important to Moody. There were, as he said, three great facts foretold in Scripture.

1. D. L. Moody, "The Second Coming of Christ," in *The Gospel Awakening*, edited by L. T. Remplap (Fairbanks: Palmer, 1883), p. 666.
2. Emma Dryer, letter to Charles Blanchard, January 1916, p. 2, Moody Archives.

One was that Christ should come the first time, as He did at Bethlehem. A second was that the Holy Spirit should come, which occurred at Pentecost. And a third was that the Lord will come from heaven a second time.[3]

For too long the church has ignored this third prophecy. Yet it is too important to forget. Its importance is underlined by the fact that, according to 2 Timothy 3:16, "all Scripture is inspired by God and profitable for doctrine and instruction." Not just some Scripture. As Moody put it, "If God didn't mean to have us study the prophecies He wouldn't have put them in the Bible."[4]

The prophecy of the second coming is important also because it is taught more often than several other doctrines that the church has spent much time emphasizing. Moody often said that the New Testament speaks of baptism only thirteen times, whereas it makes at least fifty references to the return of Christ.

Prophetic truth is important as well because it is a doctrine that purifies and revives the church. Moody observed: "The moment a man takes hold of the truth that Jesus Christ is coming back again to receive his friends to himself, this world loses its hold upon him; gas-stocks, water-stocks, and stocks in banks and horse-railroads, are of very much less consequence to him then. His heart is free, and he looks for the blessed appearing of his Lord, who at his coming, will take him unto his blessed kingdom."[5]

But considering the importance of prophecy in Moody's mind is only a first step in examining his significance

3. D. L. Moody, "The Return of Our Lord," in W. H. Daniels, *Moody: His Words, Works, and Workers* (New York: Nelson and Philips, 1877), p. 473.
4. Ibid., p. 467.
5. Ibid., p. 468.

as a premillennialist. What exactly did Moody affirm with consistency in his preaching?

First of all, Moody was definite on the premillennial return of Christ. There is no debate here. He believed that Revelation 20 was not to be taken figuratively. Christ would literally reign on earth for 1,000 years. The return would be characterized by two comings—one before the Millennium in a rapture and another after the Millennium in judgment and consummation.

In saying this, one sees Moody's use of literal hermeneutic in interpreting Scripture and prophecy. That emphasis was one he shared with other premillennialists and dispensationalists.

Moreover, his premillennial view reflected his own pessimism concerning the times:

> I don't find any place where God says the world is to grow better and better, and that Christ is to have a spiritual reign of a thousand years. I find that the earth is to grow worse and worse. . . .
>
> The antediluvian world was a failure; the Jewish world was a failure; man has been a failure everywhere when he has had his own way and been left to himself. Christ will save His church, but He will save it finally, by taking His people out of the world.[6]

Another thing that should be noticed about Moody's prophetic stance is his dismay at and rejection of any kind of date-setting regarding the Lord's return. "This doctrine has suffered a good deal from those who claim to be its friends because they set a time for his coming," he observed.[7] Moody also argued that "some have gone beyond prophecy and tried to tell the very day he would come. Perhaps that is one reason that people

6. Ibid., pp. 474, 476.
7. D. L. Moody, "The Second Coming of Christ," in *The Gospel Awakening*, p. 661.

don't believe this doctrine. That he is coming we know; but just when he will come we don't know. Matthew 24:36 settles that."[8]

A third observation needing to be made is that Moody's prophetic views did not keep him from concern and direct involvement in the social needs of his day. The claims made against Moody in this regard by George Marsden in *Fundamentalism and American Culture* are overstated.[9] Although Marsden is accurate in saying that Moody's pessimism and evangelistic interest made social action a secondary thing after preaching the gospel, and though it is true that Moody's emphasis was more on souls than on society, Moody was making plans for the future and was helping in the here and now, especially in the area of education.

In *Living in the Shadow of the Second Coming* Timothy Weber calls attention to a fourth aspect of Moody's premillennialism. Weber acknowledges that "at the same time Moody was expecting the return of Christ at any moment, he was also busy making long range plans for two educational institutions." To Weber, however, Moody's policy was no virtue but rather was an instance of a premillennialist practicing "inconsistent behavior."[10] Yet to Moody there was no inconsistency at all. He did not know when Christ would return. He preached as if Christ could return tonight. But he worked as if the event would be far in the future. It could be as far off as 1980 for all he knew—a day Moody once gave as a hypothetical

8. D. L. Moody, "The Return of Our Lord," in *Moody: His Words, Works, and Workers*, p. 470.
9. George Marsden, *Fundamentalism and American Culture: The Shaping of Twentieth-Century Evangelicalism, 1870-1925* (Oxford: Oxford U. Press, 1980), pp. 35-39.
10. Timothy Weber, *Living in the Shadow of the Second Coming: American Premillennialism 1875-1982* (Chicago: U. of Chicago Press, 1987), pp. 44-45.

possibility. Evangelism came first for Moody but not to the exclusion of helping others here and now.

A fifth observation regarding D. L. Moody's premillennialism is that it was a vague premillennialism, so vague that some have described it as inconclusive, "leaky," and inconsistent. It called forth from others the charge that Moody was not a dispensationalist at all.

Against the claim that Moody was not a dispensationalist can be cited the many indications that Moody was significantly influenced by dispensationalists. He often spoke of "an any moment return of Christ in a secret rapture." He believed in the restoration of Israel and at times made a distinction between Israel and the church, although he never made a hard and fast distinction. He occasionally spoke of dispensations, but not consistently.

Moreover, many of Moody's best friends were dispensationalists. C. I. Scofield, author of the *Scofield Reference Bible,* a major vehicle of dispensationalism, pastored the Northfield church that Moody attended when he visited that city, and Moody asked dispensationalists to speak in his conferences at Northfield on a regular basis. He felt a special kinship with them.

But there is other evidence that it is indeed "questionable whether the evangelist ever became a thorough going dispensationalist," even if dispensationalists from England and America helped to confirm Moody in his decision to adopt premillennialism in the 1870s.[11]

For one, in spite of the dispensational tenor of Moody's preaching, he sometimes spoke of Christ as having a present kingdom. Moody believed that the Ten Commandments of Moses' time applied to Christians

11. James F. Findlay, Jr., *Dwight L. Moody, American Evangelist: 1837-1899* (Chicago: U. of Chicago Press, 1969), p. 251.

and even wrote a book on the subject. And he did not speak of the church as a parenthesis in God's economy.[12]

In addition, as Stanley N. Gundry observes, Moody did not mention even once "a seven year interval between Christ's coming for his church and his return to inaugurate the millennial kingdom. In many references to Christ's return it sounds as if he made no distinction between a secret coming and a coming in power and glory. He never described a period known as the Tribulation, seven years in length."[13]

Moreover, it appears that Moody did not adopt the dispensational distinction of a pretribulation rapture as opposed to a posttribulation rapture. "The most that can be said," Gundry concludes, "is that Moody adopted the concept of an any moment return and some of its attendant vocabulary from the dispensationalists. But that he had a carefully thought-out and expressed dispensational distinction between a pretribulational rapture and a posttribulational coming cannot be demonstrated."[14]

It seems that from the 1880s on, when a rift grew among premillennialists concerning the time of the rapture, Moody increasingly realized an agnosticism. What Moody was sure about was that Jesus Christ could come at any moment. Beyond that, he did not take sides. At the end of his life Moody urged tolerance on this question. He said to a crowd in Boston's Tremont Temple, "Don't criticize if our watches don't agree about the time that we know he is coming. . . . We have been making

12. Stanley N. Gundry, "Ruin, Redemption and Regeneration: The Proclamation Theology of Dwight L. Moody, Evangelist," S.T.D. diss., Lutheran School of Theology at Chicago, 1975, p. 265. See also Stanley N. Gundry, *Love Them In: The Proclamation Theology of D. L. Moody,* Stanley N. Gundry, Moody Press, 1976.
13. Stanley N. Gundry, "Ruin, Redemption and Regeneration," p. 265.
14. Ibid.

out a program to tell us what is going to happen, and one who does that has a big job. . . . I don't know! I don't think anyone knows what is going to happen."[15]

As an evangelist, Moody held the view that the timing and the circumstances of Christ's return were matters on which there could be legitimate disagreement. The position one held with regard to Christ's return was not to be a test for fellowship or cooperation. And in this respect, Moody was a disappointment to his dispensationalist friends.

In all of this it is clear that Moody was not a systematizer of doctrine. His main concern as a premillennialist was not with precise formulation of doctrine or with the details of prophetic history, but rather with the urgency that Christ's return should inject into the lives and witness of believers.

If Christ could come for His church at any time, then time was of the essence. There might not be much time left! There was urgent work to be done. Moody said:

> I have felt like working three times as hard ever since I came to understand that my Lord was coming back again. I look on this world as a wrecked vessel. God has given me a lifeboat and said to me, "Moody, save all you can." God will come in judgment and burn up this world, but the children of God don't belong to this world; they are in it, but not of it, like a ship in water. The world is getting darker and darker; its ruin is coming nearer and nearer; if you have any friends on this wreck unsaved, you had better lose no time in getting them off.[16]

15. Ibid., p. 268. The material is taken from sermons quoted in *The Christian Herald,* February 23, 1910, pp. 168-69, "When My Lord Jesus Comes"; and December 21, 1910, pp. 1208-9, "When Jesus Comes Again."
16. D. L. Moody, "The Return of Our Lord," in *Moody: His Words, Works, and Workers,* pp. 475-76.

Such earnestness shook a great many people out of spiritual slumber to be sure. It gave Moody drive in his whole life's work. Even in the Student Volunteer Movement, the urgent note appeared. Its motto—"The Evangelization of the World in This Generation"—reflects the possible nearness of Christ's coming and the shortness of time to reach a lost world.

Towards the close of each evangelistic campaign, Moody's practice was to preach at least one sermon on the return of Christ. In his well-known sermon "The Return of Our Lord," he pressed the point home:

> The trump of God may be sounded, for anything we know, before I finish this sermon. . . .
>
> Now let the question go round, "Am I ready to meet the Lord if he comes tonight?" "Be ye also ready for in such an hour as ye think not, the Son of Man cometh."[17]

For a statement on Moody Bible Institute's position on premillennialism, see Appendix C.

17. Ibid., pp. 472, 477.

CHAPTER 13

D. L. Moody
and the Holy Spirit

God commands us to be filled with the Spirit,
and if we are not filled, it is because we are living
beneath our privileges.

—D. L. Moody, in "Nuggets of
Thought from D. L. Moody"

What did D. L. Moody believe about the Holy Spirit? A few have tried to link him with the charismatic movement, whereas others contend that he maintained a good distance from its theology.

As a boy, under Unitarian teaching, Moody thought of the Holy Spirit rather as an influence or an attribute of God. Even after he left the Unitarian church, it took ten years before he understood that the Holy Spirit is a Person in the Godhead. His own study of the Bible settled the question for him.

As Christians think about the work of the Spirit, some affirm that He does only one basic work of indwelling at the time of conversion. After that, they say, He works in us to the extent that we let Him control us. Others, however, maintain that there is such a thing as a "second blessing," which the Spirit wants to give believers. Moody's view stands somewhere between these two views.

For Moody, regeneration was the initial work of the Holy Spirit. If a man's nature was ruined by the Fall, then he not only needed to be redeemed from the curse of the law but also had to be renewed from the corruption of his heart. This work of renewal came when the Spirit created a new nature alongside the old.

Moody's position on regeneration was in line with Calvinistic teaching. Conversion could not be induced, as some revivalists of his day were saying. It was a supernatural work of the Spirit.

One thing the British noticed about Moody's preaching was that he did not use high pressure to win men for Christ. In the formal English church setting this helped to win the people's confidence in him. They were frightened by anything but a low key approach. There was no "anxious bench" as in the meetings of Charles Finney, only an inquirers' room. To Moody, revival was not "the right use of the right means," as Finney had said, but a miraculous work of God. "We can't scare people into repentance," Moody said. "They must be born in."

For Moody, regeneration was the beginning of a life-long indwelling of the Holy Spirit. He gives people a new nature. Their bodies become temples of the living God. The Spirit brings liberty, empowering people to break free from old ways of life. He brings love to the heart and light to the eyes. His continual indwelling testifies that a believer is sealed and secure in His redemption. Up until 1871, Moody's view of the Spirit's work did not go much beyond this.

Occasionally after some of his meetings in Chicago, two Free Methodist women would say to him, "Mr. Moody, we are praying that you may receive the enduement of the Holy Spirit." This irritated Moody, who believed they should rather pray for the people. But they persistently prayed that he would "get the power." Moody did not know exactly what they meant. Finally won over by their godly concern, he asked them to show him in the Scriptures the truth they insisted upon, and he even prayed with them for this power.

Over months, as Moody gave himself to prayer, he realized the state his heart was in. "I found I was ambitious; I was not preaching for Christ; I was preaching for ambition. I found everything in my heart that ought not be there. For four months, a wrestling went on within me, and I was a miserable man."[1]

The anointing for which he prayed finally came when Moody was on a trip to New York to raise money after the Chicago Fire. One day, while he walked along Wall Street, Moody was so overcome with God's love that he had to find a friend's home to get alone to pray. The sense of God's presence was so great that he asked the Lord to withhold His hand lest he die on the spot. The experience, Moody later said, marked a turning point in his life. From then on he didn't preach differently, but the response was greater than ever before.

How did Moody refer to this experience? He spoke of it as "a gift of the Holy Spirit for service," "a filling," "an anointing," "an unction," "an empowering for service," and "a baptism of the Holy Spirit." What mattered was not the name, but the reality of it.

Moody was convinced that much ministry is done by Christians without the power of the Holy Spirit. Such work is about as effective as "beating the air." So, he liked to distinguish between "strength" or "influence" and "power." Goliath, he said, had strength. But David had power. The Pharisees had influence, but the unlearned disciples had power.

Moody also saw a difference between the indwelling of the Spirit at conversion and this later filling with power: "The child of God who has been cleansed by the blood of Christ is a dwelling place of the Holy Ghost. But yet he may not have fullness of power."[2]

1. D. L. Moody, *Talks to Christians* (Chicago: Moody, 1958), p. 91.
2. Ibid., p. 76.

Moody noted that even Christ had to be anointed with special power for His public ministry. He also pointed to the disciples in John 20, upon whom Jesus breathed and said, "Receive the Holy Spirit."

Too many Christians, Moody thought, were living on past mercies of grace that God had given ten years ago. There was no fresh manna. Too much preaching depended upon human eloquence and mental ability and not God's power.

"There are two ways to dig a well," Moody was fond of saying. One way was to dig until you find water and then work to pump it out. Another was to go to a lower strata of earth, then strike water and watch the water rise on its own. The latter is an artesian well. "The Christians we want are those who are like artesian wells," Moody said. Their power comes from beyond themselves. It is the Holy Spirit's power.

Moody was not hesitant to refer to this empowering as "a baptism of the Holy Ghost," and at the Northfield conference he often requested that Reuben A. Torrey speak on the subject.[3]

Some teachers and ministers at Northfield were once offended when Moody spoke of "a baptism of the Holy Spirit." They took the view that after conversion there is no other special baptism. So Moody asked Torrey to discuss the matter with them. After a fruitless effort to change their thinking, Moody complained to Torrey, "Oh, why will they split hairs? Why don't they see that this is just the one thing that they themselves need?"[4]

In saying that D. L. Moody believed in a "baptism of the Holy Spirit," it is important to make several clarifications.

3. Reuben A. Torrey, *Why God Used D. L. Moody* (Chicago: Moody, 1947), p. 54.
4. Ibid., p. 55.

First, Moody did not link this empowering with speaking in tongues, as the Pentecostal movement did. As Stanley N. Gundry reminds us in his thorough study of Moody's theology, "The facts are, there is no place in the great mass of published Moody sermons and documents where he either suggested that he had spoken in tongues or where he advocated speaking in tongues."[5]

Second, Moody did not link this empowering with a belief in entire sanctification, as the nineteenth-century perfectionists. The old nature was not eradicated at conversion, but a new nature was placed alongside of it with greater power. The two natures are ever in conflict. Moody said that he himself was living proof that Christian perfectionism is false. He said that he had more trouble with D. L. Moody than with any other man!

And, finally, Moody did not limit this empowering to a second blessing alone. Rather, he saw it as a succession of empowerings for various works that God appoints us to. He said, "I believe that for every work we have to do for God, we should get new power. The strength God gave me for Chicago won't do for Boston."[6]

Elsewhere he wrote, "Someone once asked a minister if he had ever received a second blessing since he was converted. 'What do you mean,' was the reply. 'I have received ten thousand since the first.'

"A great many think because they have been filled once, they are going to be full for all time after. But O, my friends, we are leaky vessels, and have to be kept right under the fountain all the time in order to keep full."[7]

5. Stanley N. Gundry, *Love Them In* (Chicago: Moody, 1976), p. 241.
6. W. H. Daniels, *Moody: His Words, Works, and Workers* (New York: Nelson and Philips, 1977), p. 401.
7. Ibid., p. 321.

CHAPTER 14

Blessed Are
The Money-Raisers

Millions of dollars passed into Mr. Moody's hands, then they passed through; they did not stick to his fingers.

—R. A. Torrey, *Why God Used D. L. Moody*

"Blessed are the money-raisers, for in heaven they shall stand next to the martyrs."[1] So spoke D. L. Moody almost a century ago, as both the foremost evangelist and the foremost fund-raiser of his day.

As a nonprofit institution, the church is always looking for ways to gather support for its worship, service, and mission. In Old Testament times, Israel had the Lord God to make its solicitations, requiring a tithe of one's first fruits. Ever since, however, things have been more complicated.

How does the church call for finances to carry out its activities? Several approaches are employed.

One approach is to engage in prayer alone for the needs about us. In other words, we give out no information and put forth no solicitation.

A second option is to pray and provide information as to the pressing needs but to refrain from any solicitation.

A third method is to provide full information, coupled with varying degrees of solicitation. This third approach is seen in Pope Clement VI, who, in 1344,

1. John R. Mott, *Five Decades and a Forward View* (New York: Harper, 1939), p. 75.

threatened to excommunicate those who failed to give, or in recent times by Oral Roberts, who forecast dire developments if a specific amount was not received by a certain date.

The issues of fund-raising face most Christian ministries. And the way those issues are addressed has a public impact. Polls have shown that only 40 percent of Americans believe Christian fund-raising is honest. Nevertheless, in 1985 more than 37 billion dollars was collected in America for religious causes.[2]

The present sophistication of religious fund-raising —complete with computers and direct mail—is a recent phenomenon. One hundred years ago, fund-raising was primarily a one-man operation. Picture evangelist Moody just home in Northfield, Massachusetts, after an extended campaign in one of the major cities of the world. Appeal letters were typed for him by the hundreds and occasionally by the thousands—there were no photocopy machines. Moody preferred to sign the letters personally rather than to have his signature stamped. He would spread the letters throughout his office on floor and furniture so that the ink would dry. That is how Moody's son Paul remembers his father at home. In spite of how primitive it was and how much trouble it was, Moody's method proved to be an effective one that others soon imitated.[3]

For some time a debate has gone on in evangelical circles. It goes something like this: In asking people to support a ministry, should one be aggressive in raising funds, or is it more biblical and spiritual to pray and wait upon God to act? The debate is nearly complete,

2. American Association of Fund Raising Council, quoted in "Financing the Great Commission," *Christianity Today,* May 15, 1987.
3. John Pollock, *Moody* (London: Hodder and Stoughton, 1963), p. 255.

and it appears that, for good or ill, aggressiveness has prevailed. D. L. Moody probably had something to do with the outcome of this controversy. That is especially clear when we compare D. L. Moody to such contemporaries of his as George Mueller and Hudson Taylor.

Mueller is the evangelical's prototype of the passivist. He worked in Bristol, England, and founded homes for orphans. His practice was not to speak openly of financial need but to go to God in prayer about the matter. Time and again—and often right when the need was most urgent—the money for which Mueller prayed miraculously came in.

Mueller believed that it was "not enough to obtain means for the work of God, but that these means should be obtained in God's way. To ask unbelievers for means is not God's way. To press even believers to give is not God's way; but the duty and privilege of being allowed to contribute to the work of God should be pointed out, and this should be followed up with earnest prayer, believing prayer, and will result in the desired end."[4]

For Mueller, the key was in waiting on God for the annual £25,000 to provide for his 2,000 children. He spent time praying that would ordinarily go to fund-raising. He wanted to prove God's faithfulness. Once he even withheld the annual statement of his ministry, lest someone consider its information to be an appeal!

Mueller did inform the public about the progress of his work and gave account of how funds were used. But beyond providing minimal information, he did not solicit support. All he asked of his supporters was that they pray for God's provision.[5]

Hudson Taylor, missionary statesman to China, was another contemporary of Moody. As founder of the

4. A. T. Pierson, *George Mueller of Bristol* (James Nisbet, 1912), p. 440.
5. Ibid., p. 82.

China Inland Mission, Taylor was burdened to recruit workers for the missionary enterprise.

Like Mueller, Taylor had as one of the faith principles of the mission the rule that no appeals for money be made. He wanted to sustain the work by prayer alone. In an attitude that is almost incomprehensible in our day, Taylor wanted to avoid diverting funds from other, older benevolent societies. Subscription lists were out. "The apostolic plan," said he, "was not to raise ways and means but to go and do the work, trusting His promise who said, 'Seek ye first the kingdom of God and his righteousness and all these things shall be added unto you.' "[6] For Taylor, God's work done in God's way would not lack God's supply.

Practically speaking, this meant that if there was a need, Taylor would pray and tell others about that need. He was more aggressive than Mueller in announcing his needs. For example, in the First Occasional Paper of the mission in 1866, the exact amount of the need was specified. Hudson Taylor thus went a step further than Mueller: he believed in and practiced "full information, but no solicitation."[7]

Moody differed from these two evangelical giants, and he knew it. Pollock writes that Moody had a slight suspicion of such enterprises run in faith without an appeal. He did not understand them. For him, faith meant doing something as well as believing something. He said, "I show my faith when I go to men and state to them the needs of the Lord's work and ask them to give to it."[8]

And ask he did.

If Mueller practiced minimal information and no solicitation, and if Taylor stood for full information and

6. Dr. and Mrs. Howard Taylor, *J. Hudson Taylor* (Chicago: Moody, 1965), p. 175.

7. Ibid., p. 176.

8. Pollock, *Moody,* pp. 254-55.

no solicitation, then D. L. Moody stood for both full information and full solicitation. This aggressiveness towards raising funds was startling to some in the evangelical orbit. In fact, the Moody Bible Institute today differs from its founder by practicing full information coupled with only gentle solicitation.

The question inevitably arises as to why D. L. Moody was so different. Two factors might explain it. The first is that D. L. Moody was himself a former businessman. In an insightful doctoral dissertation written by James Howell Smith, *Honorable Beggars: Middle Men of American Philanthropy,* the author describes a conversation that took place in 1898. A successful Wall Street businessman was asked, "How is it that while you and other men like you are all but inaccessible, fenced in by closed doors and polite, but immovable secretaries, D. L. Moody can see you at any time?" The financier replied, "He is one of us."[9]

Smith reminds us that by inclination and by training, D. L. Moody was primarily a businessman. At an early age he left home and moved to Boston, where he entered business by selling shoes in his uncle Samuel's shoe store. Selling excited Moody. Whereas other salesmen waited for people to come to them, Moody went into the streets after customers. Early on, he set a goal of earning $100,000, which in those days was worth much more than it would be now.

As Moody gained experience, his wages and the opportunities at the Boston shoe store seemed too small. At that point Moody decided to move to Chicago, where another uncle lived. In 1856 that uncle helped him secure a job in a Chicago shoe store. Within a short time of his arrival in the prairie city, Moody's goal of $100,000 seemed within reach.

9. James Howell Smith, "Honorable Beggars: The Middlemen of American Philanthropy," Ph.D. diss., The University of Wisconsin, 1968, p. 52.

At that point, however, Moody started to take his Christian faith with greater seriousness. He began to divide his time between business and church work. John V. Farwell, a successful Christian businessman, became Moody's model. The only problem was that Moody's outreach to the children of Chicago through Sunday school had so captured his attention that he sensed God calling him to devote all his talent and time to the work. And what was his primary talent? It was salesmanship—a persuasive, practical-mindedness, backed by abundant energy and an earnest heart.

Moody was a businessman who entered the gospel ministry—not a gospel minister who only later took on business tasks. He thus brought a whole different mindset to the work of evangelism.

A second way Moody differed from his contemporaries with respect to fund-raising was in his belief that it was highly honorable to raise money for a worthy cause. Moody believed that to beg even a nickel for oneself was dishonorable but to beg a fortune for others was of great significance.

And yet Moody did not approach fund-raising the way some of his contemporaries did, who saw it as a sport like trout fishing. Nor did he promote the "flinch system"—a technique where the solicitor keeps increasing the amount required until he sees the donor flinch.

For what projects did Moody solicit funds? In the early days he solicited funds for his Sunday school class. Encouraged by his friend and then patron John Farwell, Moody raised $20,000 in 1863 to erect a building for his school.

Next, Moody took interest in the YMCA, which at the time was primarily an evangelistic association. Moody raised money for three Chicago halls of that association both before and after the Chicago Fire. He also raised money for chapters outside Illinois.

In raising money, Moody sometimes issued stock certificates stating that the holder had bought shares in the enterprise and could claim his dividend by the rent charged to non-YMCA organizations that used the building's facilities. Moody's main interest, however, was that the investors knew their stock would bring larger return in heaven than on earth.[10]

One of his most noted donors to the YMCA work was Cyrus H. McCormick. Once Moody asked McCormick for $25,000, telling him that "more depends on your decision than on that of any other man. Your name will help us through. The public will think, if you take hold of it, it must succeed."[11]

In addition to raising money for the YMCA, Moody also raised a great deal of money to initiate his schools. From 1879 until his death twenty years later, his total solicitations for the three schools amounted to about $1,800,000.00.[12] In Moody's mind, the schools, the YMCA, and the church were causes worthy of his aggressive abilities.

On his British tours, Moody raised funds for buildings sponsored by the YMCA and other Christian groups in Liverpool, Manchester, Dundee, Edinburgh, Glasgow, Belfast, and Dublin. Henry Drummond, who worked with Moody in Britain, reflected, "There is scarcely a great city in England where he has not left behind some visible memorial." And again, "His progress, though great in Britain and Ireland . . . is marked today by halls, churches, institutes and other buildings which owe their existence directly to his influence."[13]

10. Ibid., p. 78.
11. Ibid., p. 79.
12. James F. Findlay, Jr., *Dwight L. Moody, American Evangelist: 1837-1899* (U. of Chicago Press, 1969), p. 319.
13. Smith, "Honorable Beggars," p. 86.

Of Moody's skills Drummond said, "Mr. Moody is the most magnificent beggar Great Britain has ever known. He will talk over a millionaire in less time than it takes other men to apologize for intruding upon his time. His gift of extracting money amounts to genius."[14]

Lyman Abbott, another friend of Moody's, said that the secret to the evangelist's success in raising funds lay in his "artless faith that all money belongs to the Lord, and that it can be had for the Lord's work if one goes about in the right way to get it."[15]

This attitude of honorable money raising was also seen in Moody's care to avoid situations that would stand, both actually and apparently, to make him gain personally. Even the royalties on his books were given to needy causes. As Drummond notes, "His appeals are wholly for others . . . for places in which he would never set foot again; for causes in which he had no great personal stake."[16]

James H. Smith concludes, "Moody, who raised hundreds of thousands of dollars for other causes, considered it wise publicly and personally to avoid the temptation of financial situations in which he himself might capitalize." Smith adds, "Philanthropists trusted Moody to recommend donations that would go completely to the charities rather than accumulate in his accounts."[17]

D. L. Moody took a more aggressive approach to fund-raising than did men such as Taylor and Mueller. He did so because he was trained to be aggressive and because he believed he could use that training to serve the Lord. He dressed like a businessman, talked like a

14. Ibid., p. 105.
15. Ibid.
16. Ibid.
17. Ibid., p. 108.

businessman, thought like a businessman, and raised money like a businessman. But his business, of course, was of another sort. He was now selling the gospel and raising funds for a cause more lasting than personal fortune.

CHAPTER 15

D. L. Moody
and Robert G. Ingersoll

What legacy [did he leave] the world? Mr.
Moody, with voice and pen helped millions to faith
in God, brought light to thousands of dark homes,
built churches, established schools and left the
light of a Christian character and manhood that
will shine to distant days.
　　　　　　　　　—A. J. King, in *The Republican*

In the year 1899, two of America's most famous public speakers—Robert G. Ingersoll and Dwight L. Moody
—were silenced by death. Moody was known as the
great evangelist. Ingersoll was known as the great agnostic. One was the spokesman for Christianity; the other, an advocate of an early form of secular humanism.
Ingersoll died on July 21. Months later, after taking ill in
November during an evangelistic campaign in Kansas
City, Moody returned to Northfield where he spent his
last days. On December 22, just before the dawn of a
new century, D. L. Moody died.

Let us consider the lives of these two men more
closely.

Robert Ingersoll was an American lawyer and ora-
tor. Settling in Peoria, Illinois, he made several unsuc-
cessful attempts to enter elected office, running for a
seat in Congress and for a term as governor. In 1867 he
was appointed Attorney General of the state of Illinois.

For more than thirty years it was Ingersoll's goal to
discredit the Christian faith on platforms throughout
America. Raised in the home of a strict Presbyterian

clergyman, Ingersoll early in life turned against his father's ways and his father's God. Instead of devouring the books on theology that lined the shelves of his home, he found sustenance in the works of such skeptics as Voltaire, Thomas Paine, and Charles Darwin. His unbelief, coupled with his remarkable oratorical skill, gave him national reputation in an increasingly pluralist American nation.

Industrialist Andrew Carnegie called him "one of the great characters of modern times and one of the great orators."[1] Playwright Oscar Wilde said of him, "Robert Ingersoll is the most intelligent man in America."[2]

Author-critic H. I. Mencken, writing some twenty-eight years after Ingersoll's death, said of him that "he drew immense crowds; he became eminent; he planted seeds of infidelity that still sprout in Harvard and Yale. Thousands abandoned their accustomed places of worship to listen to his appalling heresies, and great numbers of them never went back."[3]

The differences between Moody and Ingersoll were great, and the newspapers did not miss the significance of their almost simultaneous deaths. A writer of the *New York Journal* put it this way: "These two men were remarkable in many ways, and the work of both follows them. They were types of their times. The former [Ingersoll] illustrated the ever increasing boldness and audacity of doubt as to the Christian religion, while the latter [Moody] presented that religion with a sweetness and a hope accompanying his interpretation which have no parallel in the great agnostic."[4]

1. Andrew Carnegie, in *The Best of Robert Ingersoll,* edited by Roger E. Greeley (Buffalo, N. Y.: Prometheus, 1983), p. 152.
2. Ibid., p. 170.
3. Ibid., p. 161.
4. R. B. Marsh, "Moody and Ingersoll," *New York Journal;* as on file in the Moody Archives in Northfield, Massachusetts, at the Mount Hermon School.

Moody and Ingersoll are surely not mere artifacts of a bygone era. They are types that still are found today, even if the styles of dress have changed.

Consider first the contrast in their respective creeds. Moody's creed was defined by the New Testament gospel as articulated by evangelicals then and now. It can be summed up in three phrases: "ruin by the Fall" (a real space-time event), "redemption by the cross" (the pivotal event of history), and "regeneration by the Holy Spirit" (the divine transformation of the inner life). Here is a creed that is both supernatural in its assumption and orthodox in terms of the history of the church.

But Ingersoll had no taste for historic creeds, however orthodox. He distrusted things claiming permanence. To him, "a creed [was] the ignorant past bullying the enlightened present."[5]

Despite his aversion to creeds, Ingersoll did, at one time, sum up his view of life: "I have a creed, for this the only world of which I know anything: (1) Happiness is the only goal. (2) The way to be happy is to make others happy. (3) The place to be happy is here. (4) The time to be happy is now."[6]

Not only did Moody's and Ingersoll's basic beliefs differ, but the authorities upon which the two men stood were miles apart. Moody made constant appeal to the Bible as the authoritative Word of God. Ingersoll ridiculed the Bible. It was his opinion that "free thought will give us truth."[7]

The *New York Journal* for Sunday, November 29, 1896, carried a full page spread upon which appeared large caricatures of the two men drawn according to the

5. Robert Ingersoll, in *The Best of Robert Ingersoll*, edited by Roger E. Greeley, p. 23.
6. Ibid., p. 86.
7. Ibid., p. 100.

philosophy each followed. Under Moody's image were the headlines, "The Bible Is Truth and Life; The Famous Revivalist's Strongest Argument for Christianity." Under Ingersoll, it read, "The Bible Is a Delusion: The Best Argument Ever Advanced Against Christianity."

One contemporary of Moody and Ingersoll described their differences about the Bible as follows:

> The work of Mr. Moody's life was to know and make known the Bible as the Word of God. This was the great purpose to which he gave all the powers of his being. He believed the only hope of the world was in the gospel of Jesus Christ. To him the gospel was the power and wisdom of God. . . . In the phraseology of men, he was not a scholar, but he knew God and men, and there is no higher knowledge. Mr. Ingersoll, on the other hand, studied the Bible to ridicule it. He went about the country on this mission. He labored to pull down what all good people were trying to build up. He said, "The Bible from lid to lid is a fable, an obscenity, a cruelty, a humbug, a sham, a lie."[8]

Another area of contrast lay in their views of the basic tenets of Christian thought. In the course of his life Moody moved from denying the Trinity (as a Unitarian) to affirming it as a biblical fact. He believed in Christ as the eternal Son of God made flesh for our salvation.

Of the Trinity, Ingersoll brashly quipped, "Nothing ever can be more perfectly idiotic and absurd than the dogma of the Trinity."[9] Of God he said, "The universe is all the God there is."[10] Of Christ he said, "I do not consider it a very important question whether Christ was the

8. A. J. King, editorial, *Pittsburg Commercial Gazette*; as on file in the Moody Archives in Northfield, Massachusetts.
9. Robert Ingersoll, in *The Best of Robert Ingersoll*, edited by Roger E. Greeley, p. 72.
10. Ibid., p. 37

Son of God or not. After all, what difference does it make?"[11] And again, "Do away with miracles and the superhuman character of Christ is destroyed. He becomes what he really was—a man."[12]

Such stuff sounds commonplace today. But one has to transpose Ingersoll's thoughts into a nineteenth-century setting to grasp the boldness of his statements. In those days, doubts and denial were not publicly expressed as they are today, primarily because the culture of nineteenth-century America was so influenced by Christianity. In fact, one of the reasons Ingersoll was unelectable was because his views were too heretical for the American public. One holding such views was called an "infidel," or a "blasphemer," language seldom heard today.

Although the shock value of Ingersoll's views is gone today, the relevance is not. Ingersoll threw out Christian orthodoxy for a belief in reason—or science, as he liked to say—and progress. He was a naturalist, a man having no time for anything besides what is here and now. There is nothing more than nature, he affirmed. This is not to say that Ingersoll was insensitive to the concerns of others. The exact opposite was the case. He praised the morals of Christ but threw out all that was miraculous about His life. He said, "The good part of Christianity—that is to say: kindness, morality—will never go down. The cruel part ought to go down. And by the cruel part, I mean, the doctrine of eternal punishment—of allowing the good to suffer for the bad —allowing innocence to pay the debt of guilt. So the foolish part of Christianity—that is to say the miraculous—will go down. The absurd part must perish."[13]

11. Ibid., p. 14.
12. Ibid., p. 60.
13. Ibid., p. 15.

Like many of his day, Ingersoll wanted the fruit of Christianity but not its root. He praised its humanness, but he made humanity everything to the exclusion of God. "My doctrine," Ingersoll proclaimed, "is this: All true religion is embraced in the word 'humanity.' "[14]

It was a secular humanism that he strove for. He put it this way: "Secularism is the religion of humanity; it embraces the affairs of this world . . . it is a declaration of intellectual independence . . . it means living for ourselves and each other; for the present instead of the past, for this world instead of another . . . it does not believe in praying and receiving but in earning and deserving."[15]

Ingersoll was prone to see his views as something new and progressive. They would take the place of religion in time. Moody, on the other hand, like many others, saw those so-called progressive views as very old and contorted.

The apostle Paul confronted the same kind of thinking in his day. He spoke of men who "exchanged the truth of God for a lie, and worshiped and served created things rather than the Creator" (Romans 1:25, NIV*).

When Ingersoll and others insisted that they would "not sacrifice the world [they had] for one [they knew] not of," they were mimicking an ancient insistence that Jesus faced in His day.[16] Our Lord spoke of men who were intent on gaining the whole world at the expense of losing their own souls (Matthew 16:26).

Ingersoll's "progressive" views were not only regressive and a marked departure from Christian orthodoxy, but they left a person with precious little at the end of his life. That can be seen vividly in the accounts of the death of the two famous men.

* *New International Version.*
14. Ibid., p. 86.
15. Ibid., p. 90.
16. Ibid., p. 85.

Ingersoll died suddenly. The news of his death stunned his family. His body was kept at home for several days due to the reluctance of his wife to part with it. It was eventually removed because the health of the family was at stake. Ingersoll's remains were cremated, and the public response to his passing was altogether dismal. For a man who put all his hopes on this world, death was tragic and came without the consideration of hope. The legacy of his life was one of tearing down and sowing doubt. He had used his great mental powers to deny Christianity and to take away the light and hope of others.

How different a legacy Moody left to the world. As one paper put it in a eulogy to the evangelist:

> Mr. Moody, with voice and pen helped millions to faith in God, brought light to thousands of dark homes, built churches, established schools and left the light of a Christian character and manhood that will shine to distant days.[17]

On Friday, December 22, 1899, Moody awoke to his last winter dawn. Having grown increasingly weak during the night, he began speaking in slow measured words: "Earth recedes, heaven opens before me!" Son Will, who was nearby, hurried across the room to his father's side.

"Father, you are dreaming," he said.

"No. This is no dream, Will," said the elder Moody. "It is beautiful. It is like a trance. If this is death it is sweet. God is calling me and I must go. Don't call me back."

At that point, the family gathered around, and moments later the great evangelist died. It was his coronation day—a day he had looked forward to for many years. He was with his Lord.

17. A. J. King, editorial, *The Republican* [Reading, Pennsylvania]; as on file in the Moody Archives in Northfield.

The funeral service of Dwight L. Moody reflected that same confidence. There was no despair. Loved ones gathered to sing praise to God at a triumphant home-going service. For many remembered the words that the evangelist had spoken earlier that year in New York City:

> Someday you will read in the papers that Moody is dead. Don't you believe a word of it. At that moment I shall be more alive than I am now. . . .I was born of the flesh in 1837, I was born of the spirit in 1855. That which is born of the flesh may die. That which is born of the Spirit shall live forever.[18]

These two men—Moody and Ingersoll—represented two kinds of people both in the nineteenth century and in our own time. One wanted a world with less of God and His influence. He chose to be eternally separate from all that God represented. The other, D. L. Moody, wanted more of the Person he had spent his life serving. He chose to be eternally linked with God and with all that He represented. Moody's and Ingersoll's respective moods at death's door seem to indicate that their wishes would be respected.

18. J. C. Pollock, *Moody: A Biographical Portrait* (New York: Macmillan, 1963), p. 270.

CHAPTER 16

The Tale of Two Schools

O Lord, we pray that no teacher may ever come within these walls except those who have been taught by the Holy Spirit: that no scholars may ever come here, except as the Spirit of God shall touch their hearts.

— D. L. Moody, in *So Much to Learn: The History of Northfield Mount Hermon School for The One Hundredth Anniversary*

It is a credit to D. L. Moody that the schools he began in Northfield, Massachusetts, and Chicago, Illinois, are thriving, even after 100 years. Having reviewed the educational interests of Mr. Moody and the origins of the Moody Bible Institute in earlier chapters, it is now important to consider these two works, which have long survived their founder.

Today the Northfield schools for boys and girls have merged under one board and are now called the Northfield Mount Hermon School. It is an independent, coeducational boarding school for grades nine through twelve; more than eleven hundred students are enrolled. Not only is the institution significant because of its status as a top-ranking American preparatory school (of which more will be said shortly), but it is also important because of its historical ties to Moody's life and nineteenth-century American church history.

Northfield is a lovely place to visit. The visitor is dazzled by the New England countryside. Once on campus he is confronted with many reminders of Mr. Moody's presence: his birthplace, his grave, a historical museum on his life, and his homestead for the last ten years of his life. Even the layout of the buildings gives a visitor the impression that something very significant happened there—and still does.

In another setting, far away along busy North LaSalle Drive in Chicago, stands another famous institution of Moody's making. Situated between the city's Gold Coast and the housing projects of the inner city sits the Moody Bible Institute. From the 1940s to the 1980s, when many church related institutions were leaving the city for greener suburban pastures, the leaders at MBI reaffirmed that Chicago and an urban environment were essential to their ministry. Because of the school's commitment to the city, the political leaders of Chicago have time and again made it possible for the institution to acquire land so that now Moody boasts well over ten city blocks.

Under the broad umbrella of the Moody Bible Institute one will find a vast array of innovative works of Christian outreach. Central to the enterprise is the educational branch. More than thirty-five thousand people are currently enrolled in MBI's five educational programs: undergraduate school, graduate school, extension studies (twenty-two evening school locations in six states), independent studies (correspondence school), and a Christian day school and conference ministry in Florida. In addition, Moody owns and operates an aviation school in Tennessee to train missionary pilots (about half of all missionary pilots serving in the world today were trained at Moody).

Other parts of the work include a publishing company, Moody Press, which at any given time has some eight hundred books in print (sixty new titles are released each year); a magazine, *Moody Monthly*, which has a circulation in excess of 200,000; a film division, Moody Institute of Science (in Chicago), which produces educational films about God and science as well as films of general interest; the Moody Broadcasting Network (MBN), which owns twelve stations in the United

States and produces taped programs aired on more than 430 stations world-wide.

Without question, the Chicago campus, like that of Northfield, is a beehive of activity.

But what is striking about these two projects of Mr. Moody's is not just their continued presence but also the common vision that initially brought them into being. Five principles made up that original vision:

1. To prepare young men and women for Christian service in a lay capacity.
2. To raise up a generation of Christian workers who could stand in the "gap" between the clergy and the laity of the day and who could reach out into new urban areas that were isolated from the traditional church.
3. To provide educational opportunities that were within the financial means of the poor. Moody's schools were tuition free.
4. To offer practical outlets for work. At Northfield, students were required to participate in manual work involving various skills; in Chicago, students were required to participate in inner city outreach programs.
5. To give a solid training in the Bible and toward explicitly Christian ends.

But though there were similarities in the two schools, there were also dissimilarities:

1. The Northfield Schools were situated in a beautiful rural setting, whereas the Chicago school was in the heart of a tough, brash, pulsating American city.
2. The Northfield Schools were secondary schools, whereas MBI was a post-high school institution.
3. The Northfield Schools were oriented towards the liberal arts early on, and continue to be so

today, whereas MBI was and is oriented toward specific Christian service. From the start it was more geared towards Moody's "gap men" vision, and it continues to be primarily a vocational school.

4. The Northfield Schools were led by people trained in major colleges and universities and were particularly influenced by the New England college and prep school ethos, whereas MBI was situated in a new frontier area.

In addition to the differences just listed, it appears there was a change in direction (at least in Moody's mind) in the Northfield Schools at a very early date. In the last decade of Moody's life, during the period when Henry E. Sawyer was headmaster of the Northfield Schools, a controversy broke out over the aim of the schools. A handbook prepared by Henry Rankin, a friend of Moody's who worked at the Northfield Schools, asserted that their supreme aim was to "provide academic training." Sawyer protested the emphasis thus made, saying "the Biblical course embodies the leading purpose of the school."[1] Surprisingly, Moody decided in the spring of 1890 that Sawyer—and not Rankin—should be dismissed, an action that seemed to mark a break with his earlier thinking about the direction of the Northfield Schools.

In saying that there was a shift in emphasis, it should not be construed that Moody thereby was abandoning his ideals of Christian education. As we shall see, those ideals were vital to Moody. What it did mean was that the Northfield Schools would put an increasing emphasis on academic training. When this emphasis

1. Burnham Carter, *So Much to Learn: The History of Northfield Mount Hermon School for the One Hundredth Anniversary* (Northfield Mount Hermon School, 1976), p. 57.

was combined with the influence of other New England prep schools, the direction the Northfield Schools took was a natural, logical development. In fact, Moody often looked to similar schools like Mount Holyoke and Wellesley College as models for his girls' school. Moody was a trustee of Wellesley in 1878.

As James Findlay says in his biography of Moody, with the shift in direction at Northfield, Moody's Chicago school became the place where his vision of a training center for "gap" workers took hold.

A great deal has happened since Moody's day. It has been almost one hundred years since his death, and both schools have grown and adapted to the times. Although it is impossible in this book to deal adequately with the history of each school in the years that followed Moody's death, it is possible to contrast them as they exist today and to evaluate them on the basis of D. L. Moody's original vision for the schools.

Northfield is beautiful. The two campuses that make up the Northfield Mount Hermon School are located on the Connecticut River. From the hill called "Round Top," located in the center of the Northfield campus, one can see three states—Massachusetts, Vermont, and New Hampshire. The area has all the New England charm one would expect. It is no wonder that Moody decided to live in Northfield, rather than in Chicago. Of the two physical locations, the Northfield campus was closer to Moody's heart. It was his first love, his home territory. And as writers associated with MBI, we must admit that too often this fact has been forgotten by Mr. Moody's Chicago friends.

Today the Northfield Mount Hermon School is well known as a New England prep school. As such it is one of the best in the United States. It is renowned for its academic quality and for the well-rounded four-year experience that it offers to the high school student. Its facilities are large. The school is situated on 4,000 acres and now has 164 buildings. The diversity of the program it makes available to students reflects the breadth of Mr. Moody's interests and personality, even though he never had the privilege of going to such a school himself.

Furthermore, because of its tie to Mr. Moody, Northfield still boasts of its religious goals. According to its present headmaster, the Rev. Richard Unsworth, it emphasizes the importance of spiritual cultivation of its students. It does so through a chaplaincy program, a requirement that students complete Bible and religion courses, and in other extracurricular programs it makes available. Says Unsworth, "We are trying to run a school that is as much about honor as it is about the intellect, and that teaches students to care well and care wisely for their world and the people in it."[2] In this sense, Northfield has not gone the way of much of American education, which is bent in a decidedly secular direction. The commitment at Northfield to religious values and training still holds an important place. Weighed against the standard of other American prep schools, the Northfield Mount Hermon School is striking in its quality. But the purpose of this chapter is to weigh the schools against *the vision* of Mr. Moody and to this we must now turn.

Burnham Carter has observed in his study of the Northfield Mount Hermon School that the three principles "Moody had postulated . . . for his schools: 1) low costs, 2) a work program, [and] 3) Christian commitment . . . held their force for at least half a century, and then were gradually modified to fit changing conditions and changing attitudes."[3]

In terms of tuition, fees at the Northfield Schools were low at first as a way of making it possible for the less privileged to afford an education there. A dramatic

2. *Northfield Mount Hermon Catalog: 1985-1986,* p. 4.
3. Carter, *So Much to Learn,* p. 226.

departure from Moody's vision seems to have taken place in 1969, and costs and tuition fees rose rapidly thereafter. Though today some 40 percent of the students at Northfield get financial assistance, the 1988-1989 fees for tuition, room, and board are currently $13,700, and thus out of reach for many.

As for a work program, that too was gradually phased out. Moody believed there was something about manual labor that helped build character. The academic and extracurricular programs at Northfield make life busy enough for the student, but student manual labor seems to have gone the way of the family farm.

What of Moody's stress on an explicitly Christian commitment? That too has been changed at Northfield. Under the heading of "Biblical and Religious Studies" the 1986-1987 curriculum reads:

> Students are expected to explore the nature and diversity of religious experience developing in the process attitudes of tolerance, curiosity, and sensitivity for persons and their religious beliefs and practices. It is the hope of the department that by the end of their course of study . . . students will better understand and appreciate the manifold ways in which humans have been affected by the religious experience. While we do not seek to either indoctrinate certain beliefs or to "convert" our students, neither are we purely academic discipline. Religion has to do with human commitment, and we hope to help students explore new levels of self awareness and begin the life long process of discovering patterns of meaning for their own lives.[4]

As Carter says in the opening of his book, "the [Northfield] schools have moved away from [Moody's] concept of a training ground for Christians."[5]

4. *Northfield Mount Hermon Curriculum: 1986-1987*, p. 9.
5. Carter, *So Much to Learn*, p. 15.

Although there is much about our sister school in Northfield that we appreciate and admire, as evangelicals and as people who have not abandoned the exclusivity of Jesus' claims about Himself we cannot help but lament the loss of the Christocentric focus at Northfield. The great halls that at the end of the nineteenth century thundered with the preaching of many of God's choice servants are now silent as to the gospel. The place where the call to world evangelism was so clearly articulated during the days of the Student Volunteer Movement now is more concerned about tolerance and the attitude of a pluralistic world than about the gospel of our Lord Jesus Christ, who is the same yesterday, today, and tomorrow.

When Moody dedicated Northfield's first building, he offered this prayer: "O Lord, we pray that no teacher may ever come within these walls except those who have been taught by the Holy Spirit; that no scholars may ever come here, except as the Spirit of God shall touch their hearts."[6] That prayer set forth a standard. However that standard may have been upheld at Northfield Mount Hermon, it is to the credit of the Chicago school that after one hundred years it still holds to the centrality of the Christian gospel. So many educational institutions in our country—especially the liberal arts colleges—have gone the way of Northfield. They have given up the exclusivity of the Christian message and have settled for a bland pluralism that strays from Christian orthodoxy and stirs no passion.

In a world of competing deities, Israel believed in the exclusivity of Yahweh. Israel did not talk less of the one true God for the sake of its pluralistic environment. The early Christian church faced similar social pressures. It moved in an empire that wanted to put Christ in the pantheon to make Him equal to all the other pagan

6. Ibid., p. 22.

gods from the lands the Romans had conquered. The Christians would not give up their confession that Jesus Christ is Lord of all.

It seems that the "liberal arts" of many American institutions have become so liberal that they have broken away from their unifying, Christian center. When the center is lost, the parts have nothing to hold them together. A unified view of life and knowledge becomes impossible. Universities become multiversities, a source where men are "ever learning but never coming to a knowledge of the truth" (2 Timothy 3:7).

D. L. Moody believed, as we do, that there is a center by which all things hold together. That remains Jesus Christ. He is the firm foundation for individual lives and corporate institutions.

In the year before his death Moody had this to say about his schools:

> The thought I want to present to you today is that soon these schools will be under your control. I charge you to make Christ pre-eminent in whatever you do. People keep asking me, "Have you sufficient [funds] for your schools?" My reply is that we have a rich endowment in friends. Let Christ be pre-eminent, and there will be no want of funds. Make Christ first. Make Christ the foundation and cornerstone of your lives. These schools would never have existed had it not been for Christ and the Bible. Live in Christ, and the light on this hill will shine around the world.[7]

7. Carter, *So Much to Learn*, p. 94.

CHAPTER 17

Why God Used D. L. Moody

Moody was introduced one day to a religious leader called Bewley in Dublin. "Is this young man O and O?" asked Bewley. "What do you mean by O and O?" inquired Moody's friend. "Is he Out and Out for Christ?" was the reply, and Moody never forgot it. Frequently he would talk about being "O and O."

—"Moody's Illustrations," D. L. Moody Centenary Committee, The Northfield Schools

Some might think that a book titled *Lessons from the Life of Moody*—and especially a book with a chapter called "Why God Used D. L. Moody"—cannot be taken seriously. It is just a "polemical" approach to the past. And besides, they might surmise, the past is so time-bound, its people so much the products of their own cultural environment, that their lives can be of no permanent relevance to us.

Though it is true that history does not work like a photocopy machine, there are parallels in history that make looking at the past both interesting and helpful. History sheds much light upon the present.

Some modern readers understand that. One reason so many biographies are written today is that people are curious about how others live. They want to learn something from a Trump—or an Iacocca—that might enrich them, both literally and figuratively.

Much of the Bible is written as a sacred lesson. It commends parents who instruct their children in the present by teaching them of the great things God has done in the past (see chapters 5-6 of Deuteronomy). And it also lifts up the heroes of faith as our models— men and women in God's "Hall of Fame" (see Hebrews 11).

Genesis is a history focused on the lives of six individuals and their families. Chronicles looks at the succession of kings both good and evil. The Acts of the Apostles looks at the people whom Jesus commissioned. Throughout Scripture, the thrust is much the same. Individuals can make a difference, and a study of those who have gone before us is practical in the present.

In 1923, R. A. Torrey wrote a short but challenging book titled *Why God Used D. L. Moody*. It wasn't a biography —but it would have made a great final chapter for one. The lessons Torrey drew from the life of his dear friend and colleague are valuable to us today.

The question is "why?" Why would God take such a plain man—a man born of poor parents, a country boy with little education—and use him to build His church? In posing the question, Torrey was biblical enough to admit that God gives His power to whomever He pleases. His choice is sovereign. But, Torrey added, God's blessings also have a certain conditionality about them. Those conditions are revealed in the Holy Scriptures.

Torrey's study is rightly based upon the biblical fact that in each generation God is looking for men and women to carry out His work in the world. He is searching for those who will be submissive and who are ready to act for His name's sake.

It is with these thoughts in mind that we conclude this book by presenting R. A. Torrey's rationale for God's using Moody as largely as He did.

1. D. L. Moody was fully surrendered to God.

The first reason Torrey gave for God's great use of Moody was his fully surrendered life. "Everything he was and had belonged wholly to God," said Torrey.[1]

Not that Moody was perfect. Torrey was one of Moody's closest friends. If anyone could see the evangelist's defects, he could. But after years of observation and friendship, he concluded that Moody had given himself "wholly, unreservedly, unqualifiedly, entirely to God" (Torrey, p. 10).

Once, while disputing with Torrey over something, Moody turned to his friend in defense of his position and said, "Torrey, if I believed that God wanted me to jump out of that window, I would jump" (Torrey, p. 9).

Torrey concluded that if we are to be used in our spheres as D. L. Moody was used in his, we must put all that we have and all that we are into the hands of God to be used as He will and sent where He may direct.

There are many involved in Christian work today, even as then, and they are talented, educated, and competent. Yet many stop short of absolute surrender and therefore stop short of that condition God honors by bestowing His power.

2. D. L. Moody was a man of prayer.

The second reason Torrey gave for the great power in Moody's life was that "Moody was in the deepest and most meaningful sense a man of prayer" (Torrey, p. 11).

1. R. A. Torrey, *Why God Used D. L. Moody* (Chicago: Moody, 1947), p. 8. Much of the material in this chapter is taken from this book and is used by permission. References hereafter will be given in the text.

Many people remember Moody primarily as a great preacher. According to Torrey, he was certainly that, but "he was a far greater pray-er than he was a preacher" (Torrey, p. 12). His prayers were not marked by theological sophistication, but rather by simple, trustful, definite, direct, and persistent intercession.

Moody himself said, "I would rather be able to pray like David than to preach with the eloquence of Gabriel."[2]

Moody was often confronted with large-scale problems of finance, administration, and spiritual challenge that seemed insurmountable. Yet Moody believed that nothing was impossible with God. At such times he would gather friends or students and call for a day of fasting and prayer. Sometimes they had nights of prayer. (How many ministries in America today would consider such a practice?) Moody was convinced that it was better to seek God's blessing on one's soul and work than to launch prayerlessly—and hence recklessly—into acts of ministry.

In Christian ministries today many leaders are activists. But sadly, there is often a neglect of prayer. Many hold positions of high responsibility as pastors of large churches or parachurch organizations. The engines of their ministries are running full speed. But some become so consumed with the work that they forget the source of their strength—and they burn out.

Unfortunately, the greater the visibility, the greater the danger and the harder the fall. Often that peril exists because of a dearth of prayer. Moody—the activist— prayed. And he prayed with consistency to the very conclusion of his public ministry.

2. "Moody's Illustrations," Moody Centenary Committee, Northfield Mount Hermon School, p. 7.

3. D. L. Moody was a deep and practical student of the Bible.

A third reason Torrey gave for God's use of Moody was Moody's "deep and practical [study] of the Word of God" (Torrey, p. 16).

People criticized Moody for not being a student. He was certainly not a student of the arts or sciences, even though he enjoyed reading. But he was, as Torrey says, "a profound and practical student of the one book that is more worth studying than all other books in the world put together" (Torrey, p. 17).

Torrey said of Moody:

> Every day of his life I have reason for believing he arose very early in the morning to study the Word of God way down to the close of his life. Mr. Moody used to rise about 4:00 in the morning. He would say to me, "If I am going to get in any study, I have got to get up before the other folks get up." And he would shut himself up in a remote room in his house alone with his God and his Bible. (Torrey, p. 17)

Moody himself said many times that he never met a useful Christian who was not a student of the Bible. That is the only book that comes from God with power to comfort, restore, build, and equip.

Taking what he gleaned in his personal study, Moody held the attention of large audiences around the country and plainly expounded the Scriptures. He found that the Bible was the only book with the power to "gather, hold, and bless" crowds for any great period of time.

4. D. L. Moody was humble.

A fourth secret of Moody's success was his humility. By humility is meant that he had a right estimate of himself. He looked at his life from God's perspective.

Torrey said of Moody that he was the most humble man he had ever met. That is remarkable in light of the fact that Moody lived as a public man. His work attracted international attention. Ministers and bishops followed him in the British Isles. Praise was lavished upon him in America. And reporters wrote extensively of his work.

But for all that, Moody remained gracious and unspoiled. The fame and publicity did not get to him. Spurgeon once said, "The higher a man is in grace, the lower he will be in his own esteem." That was Moody.

It was not pretense. "In his heart and mind," said Torrey, "he constantly underestimated himself, and overestimated others" (Torrey p. 29). He genuinely believed that better men were coming after him. At Northfield, he always pushed forward other men and younger men. If they were to get Moody to preach at the conference, the students had to make a special appeal.

Writing of his own day, Torrey said, "O how many a man has been full of promise and God has used him, and then the man thought that he was the whole thing and God was compelled to set him aside" (Torrey. p. 29).

Appealing to the promising young Christian workers of his time, Torrey concluded:

> Perhaps God is beginning to use you; very likely people are saying: "What a wonderful gift he has as a Bible teacher, what power he has as a preacher for such a young man." Listen: get down upon your face before God. I believe here lies one of the most dangerous snares of the devil. When the devil cannot discourage a man, he approaches him on another tack, which he knows is far worse in its results; he puffs him up by whispering in his ear: "You are the leading evangelist of the day. You are the man who will sweep everything before you. You are the coming man. You are the D. L. Moody of the day," and if you listen to him, he will ruin you. (Torrey, pp. 32-33)

5. D. L. Moody was free from the love of money.

A fifth reason Moody was so used in God's hands, Torrey said, was Moody's "entire freedom from the love of money" (Torrey, p. 33).

Although we have touched on the subject in an earlier chapter, it is important to note here that in Torrey's day, no less than our own, it could be said that "the love of money on the part of some evangelists has done more to discredit evangelistic work in our day, and to lay many an evangelist on the shelf, than almost any other cause" (Torrey, p. 36).

Certainly Moody could have been wealthy had he stayed in business. But he could also have been wealthy from his ministry. Had he taken the royalties on the hymnbooks he had published, they would have amounted to more than $1 million at that time. Nevertheless, he refused to touch them. With those profits he built the schools of Northfield and Chicago. Moody loved to raise money for God's work, but he would not let it accumulate for himself. As Torrey said, "Millions of dollars passed into Mr. Moody's hands, but they passed through; they did not stick to his fingers" (Torrey, p. 36).

6. D. L. Moody had a consuming passion for the lost.

A sixth reason Torrey gave for God's use of Moody was Moody's consuming passion for the lost:

> Mr. Moody made the resolution, shortly after he . . . was saved, that he would never let 24 hours pass over his head without speaking to at least one person about his soul. His was a very busy life, and sometimes he would forget his resolution until the last hour, and talk to someone about his soul in order that he might not let one day pass without having definitely told at

least one of his fellow mortals about his need and the Saviour who could meet it. (Torrey, p. 39)

Moody was an opportunist with this. One day while he and Torrey were paying their respects to one of Chicago's mayors, whose body was lying in state, Moody was struck by the large crowds waiting to say a final good-bye. Moody turned to Torrey and said, "This will never do, to let these crowds get away from us without preaching to them; we must talk to them. You go and hire Hooley's Opera House [which was just opposite City Hall] for the whole day" (Torrey, p. 44).

Torrey did just that. The meetings, it was said, began at 9:00 A.M. and went straight through until 6:00 P.M.

On another occasion, we are told (Torrey, p. 45), Moody walked up to a perfect stranger on a Chicago street and asked, "Sir, are you a Christian?"

"You mind your own business," was the response.

Moody answered, "This is my business."

"Well," the man said, "then you must be Moody!"

Moody did not believe that evangelism was just for evangelists. He said many times, "Every Christian is a soul winner." If heaven and hell are realities, and if those without Christ are truly lost, as Moody believed, then it was the duty of Christians everywhere to take their theology seriously and proclaim the good news to all men with that same consuming passion.

7. D. L. Moody was endued with power from on high.

The seventh key element in God's use of Moody was that Moody had a definite empowering by the Holy Spirit for his work. Torrey called that empowering "the baptism of the Holy Ghost."

As Will H. Houghton said in the foreword to Torrey's book,

Perhaps if Dr. Torrey lived in our day, and saw some of the wild fire in connection with that expression, he would use some other phrase. But let no one quibble about an experience as important as the filling with the Spirit.

The tragedy is that so many [who oppose this doctrine] are technically correct and spiritually powerless. What remains for Christians everywhere is the exhortation of Ephesians 5:18—"Be filled with the Spirit."

In his early days Moody had the reputation of a hustler, but not in the bad sense of the word. He was simply a man with "a bias for action." He was restless to do something for God. He often worked in the power of his own abilities but had no supernatural edge on what he did. God's blessing was not the characteristic mark of his work.

Torrey rightly identified Moody's experience of empowerment as he walked down Wall Street in New York City—an experience to which we have already made reference—as the turning point of his public ministry. There was a tremendous empowering that day, and it preceded the beginning of his unique ministry in Great Britain.

Although R. A. Torrey occasionally promoted that event as a kind of second conversion experience, regardless of what we make of his explanation it is a biblical fact that God does empower His people for service.

Sometimes that empowerment takes place as a one-time special empowering. Another form it takes is that of daily or moment-by-moment empowering. But just as God's assignments are many, so are His empowerings. And for this reason, "filling" appears to be the better description.

Torrey recalls in his book how, on July 8, 1894, more than four hundred students gathered at the Northfield Conference. At the end of the week they met on a mountaintop for a time of discussion and prayer. Moody said, "Young men, I can't see any reason why we shouldn't kneel down here right now and ask God that the Holy Ghost may fall upon us [and he included himself again] just as definitely as he fell upon the apostles on the day of Pentecost. Let us pray." (Torrey, p. 59)

Torrey said that as they prayed the Holy Spirit "fell upon us," and they all experienced a special visitation. Call it baptism if you will, or call it, as we prefer, filling. The point is that God uses those who are open to and anxious for His enabling strength. That is what gives a man or woman Godspeed in the work of the gospel.

These, then, are the answers R. A. Torrey gave to the question, "Why did God use D. L. Moody?":

Moody
  • was fully surrendered
  • prayed abundantly
  • was a deep and practical student of the Bible
  • was humble
  • was free from the love of money
  • had a consuming passion for the lost
  • was endued with power from on high

Do we aspire to be used by God, to be pliable in His hands and ready for His work? Then let us see how we measure up against this simple checklist of readiness for the mighty work yet to be done.

General Time Line
of D. L. Moody's Life

1837 Born, February 5, fifth child of Edwin and Betsy Holton Moody.

1850 Left school to go to work.

1854 Moved to Boston to work in his uncle's shoe store; joined the YMCA.

1855 Converted through the work of his Sunday school teacher, Edward Kimball.

1856 Joined the Mount Vernon Congregational Church, Boston.
Moved to Chicago and joined the Plymouth Congregational Church.

1858 Organized the North Market Hall Sabbath School.
Met Emma Revell at Wells Street Baptist Mission.

1859 Traveled as Salesman for Buel, Hill and Granger.

1861 Gave up business to become an independent city missionary. Began services for soldiers in military camps during Civil War.

1862 Elected life member of YMCA; married Emma C. Revell on August 28.

1863 Appointed missionary of the YMCA.

1864 Helped organize the Illinois Street Church, later called the Chicago Avenue Church; in 1900 called the Moody Memorial Church.

1865 Enrolled as a student in the newly organized Baptist Theological Seminary.

1866 Elected president of the Chicago YMCA.
Played a leading role in raising money for the first YMCA building in America.

1867 Visited Great Britain to meet religious leaders and to preach; visited Paris.

1870 Met Ira D. Sankey, song leader at the International YMCA Convention.
Visited Great Britain (second visit). Attended conference of Christian workers in Dublin.

1871 The Chicago Fire; the YMCA building, Moody's house, and the Illinois Street Church destroyed.
Filled with the Spirit in New York.
Dedicated Northside Tabernacle.

1872 Visited Great Britain (third visit).

1873 Visited Great Britain (fourth visit) and conducted first great campaign.
Sacred Songs and Solos used for the first time.

1874 Continued meetings in England, Ireland, and Scotland.

1875 Conducted Great London Campaign (March 9—July 16; 85 meetings; 2,500,000 people).
Held first large city campaigns in America—Brooklyn and Philadelphia.

1876 Dedicated Chicago Avenue Church.
Bought home in Northfield.

1879 Opened Northfield Seminary (school for girls).

1880 Held first Northfield Summer Conference.

1881 Opened Mount Hermon School for Boys.
Visited England (fifth visit).

1882 Held meetings in Great Britain; preached four weeks in Paris; rested in Switzerland.

1883 Returned to America in April; to London for eight months' campaign (sixth visit).

1886 Student Volunteer Movement organized.

1888 Visited Great Britain (seventh visit).

1887 Chicago Evangelization Society founded. Later called the Chicago Bible Institute; and later, in 1900, called the Moody Bible Institute.

1891 Visited Great Britain (eighth visit).

1892 Visited Europe and the Holy Land; continued revival meetings in Great Britain.
Experienced sea accident on way home.

1893 Great campaign held at Chicago World's Fair.

1894 Established The Moody Bible Institute Colportage Association, called Moody Press in 1941.

1895 Started work for men in prisons.

1896 Elected president of the International Sunday School Association.

1898 Served on national committee to start Army YMCA work during Spanish American War.

1899 Suffered breakdown of health in Kansas City in November; died in Northfield, Massachusetts, December 22.

Evangelistic Campaigns of D. L. Moody

1873-5 Fourth visit to Great Britain and first great campaign. Meetings in many cities in England, Scotland, and Ireland, closing with a great campaign in London, March 9 to July 11, 1875. An estimated 2,500,000 people attended during the course of 85 meetings.

1875 First large city campaigns in America; in Brooklyn in October and in Philadelphia from November 21 to January 16, 1876.

1876 Philadelphia, New York, Chicago, Nashville, Louisville, St. Louis, Kansas City, Chicago—October to January, 1877.

1877-9 Chicago, Boston (twice), Mexico, Canada; Burlington and Montpelier in Vermont; Concord and Manchester in New Hampshire; Providence, R.I., Springfield, Mass., Hartford, Conn.; Baltimore—October 14 to May 25, 1879 (270 sermons preached).

1880 Six months of meetings in St. Louis; meetings in Pacific Coast cities.

1881-3 Fifth visit to Great Britain.

1883-4 Sixth visit to Great Britain.

1885 Alabama, Virginia, North Carolina, and other locations.

1886 Atlanta, University of Virginia, New Orleans, Houston, Wheeling, Washington, New York.

1887 Four months' campaign in Chicago.

1888 Pacific Coast cities, including Victoria and Vancouver in British Columbia.

1888-9 Seventh visit to Great Britain.

1891-2 Eighth visit to Great Britain.

1893 Great campaign at Chicago World's Fair (May-November).

1894 Washington, Providence, Lowell, Toronto, Birmingham, Richmond, Scranton, Wilkes-Barre.

1895 New York, Philadelphia, Atlanta, Boston, Worcester, Bangor, Dallas, Mexico City and Toluca in Mexico, Fort Worth, Rochester, N.Y.

1896 Plainfield, N.J., New York (November-December).

1897 Boston (January-February), Cincinnati, Ottawa, Winnipeg, St. Louis, Brandon (Canada), Pittsburgh, Chicago.

1898 Toledo, Montreal, Tampa Bay; Hopkinsville and Louisville, Ky; Leadville, Florence, and Boulder, Colo.

1899 Las Vegas; Phoenix and Tucscon, Ariz.; San Diego, Santa Rosa, and San Francisco in California; Salt Lake City; Bridgeport; Kansas City; meetings interrupted by breakdown in health.

Further Notes on Premillennialism

Reuben A. Torrey, close associate of Moody and the second president of the Moody Bible Institute, stated, "The latter truth [the second coming of Christ] transformed my whole idea of life; it broke the power of the world and its ambition over me, and filled my life with the most radiant optimism even under the most discouraging circumstances." Dr. Torrey was asked, "Is not the doctrine of Christ's personal and near coming one of practical power and helpfulness?" He replied, "It is transforming the lives of more men and women than almost any doctrine I know of."[1]

James M. Gray, third president of Moody Bible Institute, explained how the doctrine of the second coming of Christ influenced his life:

> There are at least five things which this hope effected in my life . . . it awakened a real love and enthusiasm for the study of every part of God's Word; it quickened my zeal in Christian service, especially in foreign missions; it delivered my mind from an overweening ambition for worldly success and the praise of men; it developed patience and quietness in the face of unjust treatment; and it broke the bonds of covetousness and set me free to give of my substance to the Lord.[2]

The Moody Bible Institute is a theological institution and as such outlines its doctrinal stance in its bylaws. Article 5 of its constitution states:

> The Church is an elect company of believers baptized by the Holy Spirit into one body; its mission is to witness concerning its Head, Jesus Christ, preaching the gospel among all nations; it will be caught up to meet the Lord in the air ere He appears to set up His Kingdom (Acts 2:41; 15:13-17; Eph. 1:3-6; 1 Cor. 12:10,11; Matt. 28:19,20; Acts 1:6-8; 1 Thess. 4:16-18).

Moody Bible Institute faculty member Louis Goldberg offers a summary of Article 5 in the booklet "Here We Stand":

> We believe in the second coming of Christ. His return from heaven will be personal, visible and glorious, a blessed hope for which

---

1. Reuben A. Torrey, "He Is Coming," in *Gospel Herald,* September 1, 1962.
2. William Culbertson, "Christ the Hope of the World," p. 11.

we should constantly watch and pray (Titus 2:13; Acts 1:11; Rev. 1:7; Zech. 14:4).

The second coming of Christ will consist of two major events. Before He will appear to initiate His kingdom on earth, He will come in the rapture. It is this event that will resurrect the dead in Christ and translate the living Christians to be with Him forever, thereby removing from the earth His waiting Church to meet the Lord in the air (1 Thess. 4:14f; 1 Cor. 15:51-54).

In this resurrection, those who have died in Christ will have their redeemed souls and spirits united with a body similar to Christ's glorified body. Christians living at the time of this event will not die, but their bodies will be changed to be like that of Christ (1 John 3:2). It is an encouragement for consistent living (1 John 2:28) as well as a comfort (1 Thess. 4:18). This resurrection is to take place at the last day, but no man knows the day or hour (John 6:39; Matt. 24:36).

At that time, Christians will be brought before the judgement seat of Christ, and Jesus Christ as Judge will determine their rewards on the basis of the works they have accomplished (Rom. 14:10-12; 2 Cor. 5:10). This is not a judgement to determine the salvation of the Christian, but rather the reward of all Spirit led labor on His behalf (1 Cor. 3:9-15).

During the time of the judgement seat of Christ in heaven, there will be a period on earth known as the "great day of His wrath" (Rev. 6:17), "the great tribulation," (Rev. 7:14) and the "time of Jacob's trouble" (Jer. 30:7). It is a time of unprecedented woe on earth that will affect Israel and all nations. While God will have His witnesses in this period (Rev. 7), it will nevertheless be a time of His wrath in righteous judgements to subdue nations and men (Isa. 2:12; Matt. 24:21, 22; many sections in Rev.). The purpose of this period of horror is to prepare Israel for her Messiah (Zech. 12:2, 3; 14:1-3) and to remove all rebellion against Christ by unbelieving men and nations at the second coming of Christ to the earth (Rev. 16:14, 16; 19:19).

In this latter event, Christ comes with the hosts of heaven as well as the Church (Rev. 19:7-9, 14; 1 Thess. 3:13) to establish the Messianic kingdom on earth (Zech. 14:9; Rev. 19:15,16) that will last for a thousand years (Rev. 20:2, 4-6). At that time there will be the final consignment of the Antichrist, the binding of Satan (Rev. 19:20; 20:1-3), and the judgement of the nations and their representatives (Joel 3; Matt. 25). Israel will ultimately be restored to her land, never more to be removed (Amos 9:15; Ezek. 34:28), and be prominent among the nations. The reign of Christ will be firm, but it will be with equity (Ps. 2:9; Isa. 11:4). It will be a kingdom characterized by material blessing since the curse upon the earth will be removed (Rom. 8:19-21). There will also be great spiritual blessing as there will be unprecedented opportunity to hear the truth of God and become a child of God.

The Messianic kingdom will close with apostasy and rebellion (Rev. 20:7-9) as God crushes the uprising in the last battle of the ages. Satan will be deposed to the lake of fire (Rev. 20:10). The soul and spirits of all ages who had rejected the Word of God and descended into hades will be resurrected in their bodies at the final day of the great white throne judgement (Rev. 20:11-13). There they will be judged and cast into the lake of fire, the place where they will suffer final everlasting punishment (Rev. 20:14, 15; Mark 9:48).

After the great white throne judgement there will be a final renovation of the heavens and earth to make it anew and usher in the eternal state (Isa. 66:22; 2 Pet. 3:13). There will be a new Jerusalem (Rev. 21:2, 3), all new provisions (Rev. 22:1, 2) and the everlasting presence of God (Rev. 22:3-5) among all the redeemed.[3]

3. Louis Goldberg, subsection "The Second Coming of Christ," p. 19, in "Here We Stand."

Selected Bibliography

Findlay, James F., Jr. *Dwight L. Moody: American Evangelist.* Chicago: U. of Chicago Press, 1969. A scholarly study of Moody's life placing Moody within the social, cultural, and theological developments of his day.

Gundry, Stanley N. *Love Them In: The Proclamation Theology of D. L. Moody.* Chicago: Moody, 1976. Provides an excellent overview of Moody's theology and gives a thorough bibliography of Moody studies and dissertations.

Moody, Paul. *My Father.* Boston: Little, Brown, 1938. Written by Moody's younger son. Now out of print.

Moody, William R. *The Life of D. L. Moody.* New York: Macmillan, 1930. Presently published by Barbur and Company, Westwood, N. J., 1985. Reprint of the large biography of Moody by his older son published in 1930 by the Macmillan Company.

Pollock, J. C. *Moody: A Biographical Portrait.* New York: Macmillan, 1963. Published in England by Hodder and Stoughton under the title *Moody: Without Sankey,* this book is a sympathetic study of Moody's rise as an evangelist.